Pirates of Colonial Newport

Gloria Merchant

THE
History
PRESS

Published by The History Press
Charleston, SC 29403
www.historypress.net

Back cover images courtesy of the Newport Historical Society.

First published 2014

Manufactured in the United States

ISBN 978.1.62619.250.8

Library of Congress CIP data applied for.

To Jack

Contents

Acknowledgments

Sincere thanks to my History Press team: Jeff Saraceno for your enthusiastic launch, Katie Orlando for casting me off and Krista Slavicek for helping me to navigate.

Thank you Redwood Library for your outstanding staff, incomparable collection and exceptional historical images. I'd particularly like to thank Whitney Pape, Special Collections librarian and Robert Kelly, Collections librarian.

I owe additional thanks to Tara Ecenarro of the Newport Art Museum for your help beyond the call of duty.

Thank you to the Newport Historical Society for your unique and comprehensive research library and photo archives. I extend additional gratitude to Jennifer Robinson for your tireless help locating images and to Bert Lippincott for your encyclopedic knowledge of Newport's history and boundless enthusiasm for sharing the same.

Thanks also to the Newport Public Library for your Newport Room and relentless reference librarians.

Thank you to Salve Regina University for providing access to America's historical newspapers.

I'd like to thank my friends at the Providence Art Club for your help in a crunch.

A special thanks to Ginny Saunders and Frances and Alfred Lopes for insights into Conanicut's history that only locals can provide. Thanks also to Sue Maden and Rosemary Enright of the Jamestown Historical Society.

Thank you to Rhode Island Historical Society for your knowledge, collection and super staff.

Thanks to Pamela Gasner at the Block Island Historical Society for your informative tour of the island.

Thank you to Susan Anderson, Roz Kopit, Adriane Scola-Jones, Alision Quinlan and Helene Scola. Your insightful comments helped me keep the story of Newport's pirates on course.

Additional thanks to Helene Scola for your friendship, support and wicked good photos.

A special thanks to James Hattendorf for generously sharing your knowledge of Trinity Church and admiralty courts.

I want to thank Tim Cranston, North Kingstown town historian and worthy descendant of the "Govnah," for your time, knowledge and unique perspective.

Thanks also to my friend and Newport neighbor Maggie Cousineau-Arndt for loaning me your rare book about Newport's Point.

Thank you to Roswell for allowing your photograph to be included.

Thank you to Terri Davis-Merchant and Steven Munger for sharing your linguistic skills.

Boundless thanks to my husband, Jack, for technical support and manuscript critique. I also have to thank you for your (mostly) cheerful willingness to share my attention with rogues, scoundrels, wicked and ill-disposed persons.

Introduction

R ed Sea pirates sailed out of Newport Harbor, attacked Muslim ships, returned to Newport, sold plunder and spent foreign gold. Privateers who dabbled in piracy, pirates who pretended to be privateers and outright pirates all weighed anchor in Newport Harbor. Liars, thieves, murderers and rapists drank at local taverns. Who were those men? What drove them to piracy? Why did Newport's citizens welcome them? Why did those same citizens turn against them?

Newport's piratical past and the answers to those questions lay buried like treasure. Hints exist in place names like Pirates' Cove and Pirates' Cave. Stories of Kidd's buried treasure persist. Municipal workers dug up gold, silver and jewels while laying water pipes in nearby Jamestown. In the mid-twentieth century, an ancient chest appeared and then disappeared under Newport's cliffs. Ghost stories about executed pirates haunting their watery graves make for excellent telling.

In order to unearth the history behind the legends, I plundered colonial records, depositions, newspaper accounts, correspondence and reports by royal officials. I learned about commerce, England's endless wars and greed and corruption on both sides of the Atlantic. The treasure I unearthed revealed the turbulent reality of life in colonial Newport.

Many of Newport's fathers, husbands, sons and brothers sailed under the black flag, but Newport's pirates did not always fit the swashbuckling stereotype. They often returned home, bought property, started businesses, held public office, married, raised families, attended church and died peacefully in their beds.

Map of Rhode Island detail by John Reid, 1796. Newport is located in Rhode Island.
Courtesy of the Redwood Library & Athenaeum, Newport, Rhode Island.

The first pirates to sail out of Newport carried privateering commissions during England's war against the Dutch in 1652. New Netherland justifiably condemned them.

From the mid-seventeenth to the mid-eighteenth centuries, Parliament passed a series of Navigation Acts designed to make English colonies dependant on London for European goods and keep the balance of trade in England's favor. A combination of smuggling and piracy leveled the playing field.

By 1698, representatives to the king accused Rhode Island's government, whose capital was Newport, of conniving with smugglers and favoring pirates. They were right. A business partnership existed between Newport's pirates, merchants and colonial government. Local mariners plundered Red Sea shipping, brought luxury goods home and sold them to Newport merchants and private citizens at bargain prices. The government provided the outlaws safe haven for a fee. Pirates liberally spent foreign gold and silver currency in the cash-starved colony. Newporters welcomed them.

Newport's relationship with pirates and its attitude toward them changed in the early eighteenth century. When Queen Anne's War ended, in 1714, many unemployed English and Anglo-American sailors and privateers became pirates. They spent the winter freebooting in the Caribbean and passed the summer plundering along the Atlantic coast. Colonial shipping suffered heavy losses and barbaric treatment at their hands. Newport wanted no part of them.

Once Newport's growing and prosperous shipping fleet was on the receiving end of piracy, it was pleased to cooperate with London's pursuit of pirates, but a different form of robbery threatened Newport's economy. Taxation without representation stole profits, and England's enforcement ships stole property.

Rum was Newport's "cash crop." Rhode Island merchants traded rum for African slaves, traded slaves for Caribbean molasses, took the molasses home to make rum and returned to Africa. That triangle trade created fortunes. Parliament levied heavy taxes on molasses imported from non-English sources with the 1733 Molasses Act. When Rhode Island merchants needed more molasses than English plantations could provide, French molasses joined the list of goods smuggled into Newport.

During the late eighteenth century, England stationed warships in Newport Harbor to seize contraband and collect taxes. Its enforcement ships harassed everything from small coastal traders to ocean-going merchant vessels. Newporters resented the heavy-handed approach of His Majesty's officers. They rioted, attacked enforcement ships and torched one. When Rhode Islanders torched a second ship, the *Gaspee*, London branded the perpetrators pirates and called for their arrests. Those pirates became part of a formidable privateering fleet that helped win the American Revolution.

The story of Newport's pirates began with war and ended with revolution. It is a rich history and the stuff of legends.

1

The Players

Colonial Newport's docks spawned pirates, privateers and smugglers. It was often difficult to separate the three occupations.

Pirates

Pirates attacked everything from canoes to well-armed merchant ships. They did not, however, attack fellow pirates. International pirate crews considered themselves to be a brotherhood. They addressed one another as Brother Pirate and referred to themselves as Brethren of the Coast. Group loyalty led many to exact revenge on cities that executed their brethren by killing captains and destroying ships from those harbors. Pirates were violent, battle-hardened thugs. Images of them armed to the teeth with pistols, knives and cutlasses are no exaggeration. They lived hard, drank hard and died, for the most part, young.

Many sea rovers received their training and experience in either the Royal Navy or the merchant marines. They knew what they were doing. They also knew that life on a pirate ship was better than life on naval or merchant ships. Britain's rigid class system extended its abuses to its naval and merchant fleet. Sailors drifted in from Britain's lower classes while officers cruised in as sons of privilege. Discipline on board included brutal beatings that could result in disability or death. Officers ate and drank

The Buccaneer Was a Picturesque Fellow. Howard Pyle illustration. *From* Harper's Monthly, *December 1905.*

well, but the crew did not. Common sailors earned little and captains often withheld the crews' wages to discourage desertion. Sailors routinely deserted and, occasionally, mutinied with piratical intent. Pirates blamed abusive captains and life in His Majesty's service for their career moves as often as they blamed hard liquor.

Pirates governed themselves democratically and distributed plunder equitably. Crews voted on where to sail and what ships to attack. Crews also voted captains in or out of command. The captain's authority was absolute only during battle. Captains shared sleeping quarters with their men and ate in the common mess. Pirates did not tolerate abusive captains. They would be voted out of office and marooned.

The workload for pirate crews was lighter than for merchant crews. In *Under the Black Flag*, Cordingly explained that twelve crewmen typically manned a one-hundred-ton merchant ship. Eighty or more pirates manned vessels of comparable size.

Since pirates could not easily purchase boats or fit out legally, they stripped captured vessels of everything useful, including guns, ammunition, rigging, tackle and sails. Pirates added desirable prizes to their fleet and burned or scuttled undesirable ships. Released prisoners might have been allowed to make their way home in their stripped vessel. Pirates often stripped prisoners as well. Gentlemen of fortune had an eye for fine clothing.

Pirates fought to the death to avoid capture but preferred that their prey surrender with a minimum of violence. Once the Jolly Roger was hoisted, they relied on their ferocious reputations and superior numbers to intimidate the opposition. Aside from not wanting to risk injury or death, pirates did not want to damage the vessel under attack. A sunken prize was of no value, and a badly damaged ship could not be added to their fleet.

Treatment of prisoners ranged from civil to sadistic. Pirates treated a ships' captain according to how well the captain treated his crew. Prisoners who offered little or no resistance could be allowed to sail away unharmed. If the prize was hard won, its surviving crew risked being slashed with cutlasses, tortured and/or murdered. Particularly brutal treatment, including the cutting off of ears, lips and noses, was used to force prisoners to reveal the location of treasure.

Pirates always invited prisoners to join their crew. Many voluntarily signed the ship's articles, rules governing conduct, compensation and punishment. Men who possessed valued skills, such as doctors, carpenters and coopers (barrel makers), would be forced to join. Musicians would also be forced. Pirates enjoyed entertainment, plus, drumming and horn blowing during battle helped to demoralize the opposition.

Pirates often referred to themselves as privateers. The job description was partially the same: attack merchant ships and steal their cargo.

Privateers

Between 1652 and the American Revolution, England was at war more often than it was at peace. The Royal Navy could not spare men of war to defend the colonies and disrupt enemy commerce along the Atlantic coast. It needed privateers.

England and its enemies commissioned privately owned, armed vessels to augment their navies. The practice expanded their fighting fleets for free. It was a win/win for warring nations. What was in it for the privateers? Money.

Privateers brought captured enemy warships and commercial vessels into port to have them condemned as legitimate prizes by an admiralty court. The terms of the commission determined how proceeds from the sale of a vessel and its contents would be divided. Captains, crews, owners and the Crown received a percentage of the total. Captains and crews did not receive a salary. If they failed in their commission, they worked for free: no prey, no pay.

In order to obtain a privateering commission in England's colonies, a ship's captain requested a letter of Marquee and Reprisal[1] from a colonial governor. That document, acquired for a fee, defined the purpose and duration of the commission. It also stated what percentage of the income would be received by the privateer's captain, crew, owners and the Crown. Colonial governors could accept gifts but not a share of profits.

Money could be made even if privateers played by the rules, but fortunes could be made if they broke the rules. Privateers occasionally attacked merchant ships not at war with England. Some captains received privateering commissions to provide a veneer of legitimacy to piratical activity. Both practices dressed pirates in privateers' clothing.

A notorious example of a privateer who broke the rules was Newport's native son Thomas Tew. Captain Tew's first privateering commission was granted in good faith. His subsequent commission was obtained despite the fact that everyone knew he intended to go a-pirating in the Red Sea.

Colonial governors often granted commissions knowing that the captain had no intention of privateering against the enemy. Captains, crews and ship owners divided plunder from neutral shipping. Sponsoring governors and their colonial governments received gifts or bribes. No one arrested the privateers for piracy, but they were pirates.

Smugglers

Colonial smugglers avoided taxes and imported goods illegally. In 1651, London passed the first of a series of Navigation Acts designed to enrich Britain at the expense of everyone else, including its colonies. Colonial America viewed London's trade restrictions as obstacles to be overcome, not laws to be obeyed. The colonies relied on their merchants to sabotage Parliament's efforts to legislate and tax them into submission. Newport's merchants met the challenge.

Throughout the colonial period, Rhode Island merchants devised elaborate schemes to circumvent the law, evade London's taxes and bring illegally obtained English, West Indian and European goods into the colony. Smuggling occasionally involved open acts of piracy, privateers' selling goods embezzled from their prizes and acquiring plunder from pirates. Two Newport merchants, Benjamin Norton and Joseph Whipple, outfitted a brigantine for trade but ended up consorting with pirates instead.[2]

The demand for affordable European manufactured goods, as well as molasses for the production of rum, and the desire for profit led to colonial smuggling. Abusive tactics by the captains and crews of England's enforcement ships drove Newporters to attack them—acts of piracy that incurred London's wrath.

2

Newport's First Privateers and Pirates

A conniving bully, an opportunistic soldier of fortune and a marauding bigamist became Newport's first privateers. They were also the town's first pirates.

The Dutch War

Maritime trade was the spark that ignited war between England and Holland in 1652. Rhode Island was vulnerable. An English settlement occupied eastern Long Island, and the Dutch occupied western Long Island. London directed the colony to defend itself.

The colony of Rhode Island and Providence Plantations had two general assemblies for a short time in its early history: the Mainland Assembly included the towns of Providence and Warwick, while the Island Assembly included the towns of Newport and Portsmouth on Aquidneck Island, which was called Rhode Island. The Island Assembly organized an admiralty court to issue privateering commissions and condemn enemy prizes.[3]

Edward Hull, Captain John Underhill and Thomas Baxter obtained privateering commissions. Newport should have chosen more wisely.

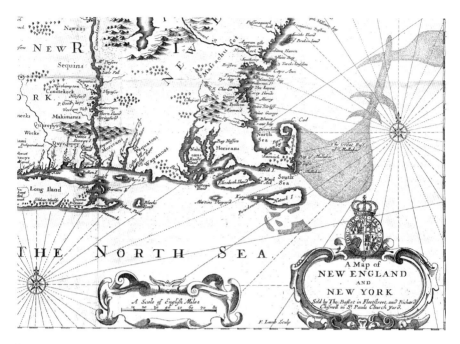

Map of New England and New York detail by John Speed, 1676. *Courtesy of the Redwood Library & Athenaeum, Newport, Rhode Island.*

Edward Hull

When Edward Hull learned that a war between England and Holland was imminent, he captured a Dutch vessel and hid it in one of Narragansett Bay's coves. After war was declared, Hull secured a privateering commission and brought his prize into Newport Harbor. The ship was condemned by Newport's admiralty court, but the Dutch captain sued. He proved that Hull acted in haste, and the decision was overturned and the captain awarded full compensation.

Hull's next seizure belonged to Thomas Baxter, another Newport privateer. Hull defended himself valiantly, if offensively, before a New Haven court. When the magistrates threatened to send Hull to London to see what Parliament thought about his privateering, Hull realized the error of his ways and promised to behave.

The privateer was, apparently, incapable of behaving, however. Hull's final capture, a French vessel, had nothing to do with the war against the Dutch.

Captain John Underhill

Captain Underhill sold his mercenary services to Massachusetts Bay Colony and the Dutch Colony of New Netherland. Both governments found reason to banish him. He moved to Newport, where he received a warm reception and a privateering commission.

Underhill's single act as a privateer was to seize a Dutch West India Company trading post on the Connecticut River. He sold his share of the conquest over the objections of Connecticut's general court. Newport realized no financial or military gain from Captain Underhill's privateering.

The Canon Shot. Willem van de Velde the Younger, 1680. A painting of a Dutch man of war firing its canon. *Rijksmuseum, Amsterdam*.

Thomas Baxter

Peter Stuyvesant, Dutch director general of the colony of New Netherland, complained about English pirates attacking Dutch and English residents.[1] Thomas Baxter commanded the pirates. After Baxter stole a barque owned by Samuel Mayo of Plymouth County, Connecticut ordered his arrest. Baxter eluded capture, continued privateering and created more enemies than friends.

Baxter's theft of a canoe belonging to a Connecticut magistrate was the last straw. A second order for his arrest caught up with him. His capture caused the only recorded casualties of the Dutch war in New England. Baxter's crew learned where he was held and assaulted the guards. One of Baxter's men was killed, and an officer was wounded in the rescue effort.

Baxter's privateering ended, but his legal problems did not. His wife claimed he had another wife in England and sued for divorce. Afterward, Bridget Baxter's ex-husband disappeared from her life and Newport's history.

The End of the First Dutch War

Newport's privateers proved to be more trouble than they were worth. The Dutch West India Company demonstrated admirable self-restraint by choosing not to attack those "pirates" out of Newport.

3

Newport's Own Thomas Tew

Thomas Tew was well born, well connected and anything but well intentioned. His business partners included Governor Fletcher of New York, pirate patron, and Captain John Avery, arch-pirate.

In its September 19, 2008 article "Top-Earning Pirates," *Forbes* magazine ranked Tew third after Sam Bellamy and Sir Francis Drake. Tew's wealth, estimated at $103 million, was well above Blackbeard's modest $12.5 million.

Native Son

Tew was related to a respected Newport family. One ancestor is listed in the colony's charter of 1663. Another family member became Newport's deputy governor in 1714. Thomas's father, also named Thomas, was probably a mariner.

Tew Goes A-Privateering

Tew arrived in Bermuda in 1691 with ambition backed by gold. He purchased a share in the sloop *Amity*. It was common knowledge that Tew had sailed on the account, a reference to piracy. That reputation was probably an asset to his résumé.

King William's War set Tew on a course of plunder and profit. In 1693, Bermuda's lieutenant governor issued a privateering commission to Tew and another captain to destroy a French factory off the African coast. When a violent storm separated both sloops, the *Amity*'s captain decided to change course.

Captain Charles Johnson's *The History of the Pirates* reported that Tew called all hands on deck and made his case to abandon their commission. Tew explained that he saw the prospect of danger, but not treasure in the venture. He preferred to risk his life for profit, not military victory. His crew agreed and chose to follow its captain on a course to "Ease and Plenty."

The Course to Ease and Plenty

Tew and his mates sailed around the Cape of Good Hope into the rich promise of the Red Sea. Merchantmen known as the Mocha Fleet traveled regularly between Surat in India and Mocha and Jidda in Arabia. Wealthy religious pilgrims traveled with servants and valuables. Merchants carried goods on the outward journey and gold, silver and jewels received for those goods on the return journey. English pirates and their patrons thought it was no sin for Christians to rob infidels. Muslim wealth beckoned.

A tall ship crossed the *Amity*'s path. It was rich and well armed. Three hundred soldiers guarded it and five additional treasure ships that followed. In spite of the odds, Tew and his crew of forty-five decided to attack. The pirates' skill and courage proved superior to that of their prey. They captured the prize without any casualties. The ship carried a fortune in gold, silver and jewels. The pirates also took as much gunpowder as the *Amity* could carry and tossed the rest overboard.

That astonishing success inspired Tew to pursue the five ships that had not yet arrived. The *Amity*'s quartermaster talked him out of it. They had treasure enough and no room to stash it. Having been overruled by his crew through their shipboard representative, Tew steered for Saint Mary's Island off the Madagascar coast.

Madagascar was an ideal pirate base. Red Sea shipping provided rich, poorly defended targets. India's Great Mogul and London's East India Company had a working relationship. Attacks against Muslim shipping

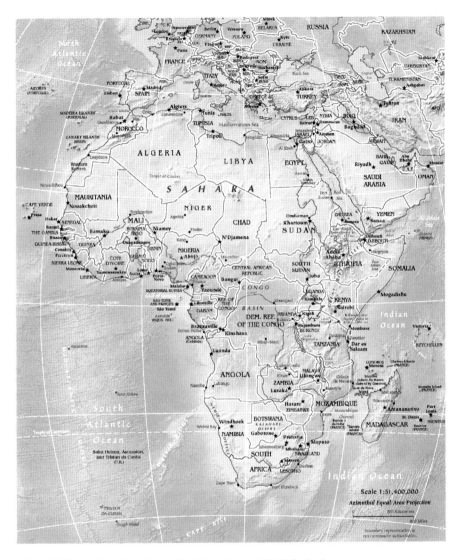

Map of Africa. *United States Central Intelligence Agency's World Factbook.*

jeopardized that relationship, but the Royal Navy was stretched too thin to protect shipping interests in the Red Sea. Pirates freebooted with abandon and brought their loot to Madagascar to trade with agents from New York. If they preferred to eliminate the middleman, they refit at Madagascar and crossed the Atlantic.

Tew's quartermaster and twenty-three of his crew members chose to stay on St. Mary's. The *Amity* sailed for Bermuda with twenty-one men.

On the way to Bermuda, Tew allegedly fell in with a pirate chief named Mission who founded a pirate colony, Libertatia, on northern Madagascar. Tew's alleged adventures in Libertatia included commanding an expedition to seize slaving ships; taking a Dutch East Indiaman, an English slaver and an Arabian treasure ship; charting the coast of Madagascar; fending off a Portuguese attack; and becoming admiral of the pirate fleet. However, Tew left Bermuda in 1693 and arrived in Newport in the spring of 1694. There was not enough time to have had the extended adventure with Mission. Furthermore, Mission's entire story is believed to be a fiction perpetuated by DeFoe writing as Captain Johnson in *A General History of the Pyrates*.

What is known for certain is that when Tew set out for Bermuda, a storm forced him to steer for Rhode Island. Newport received the news of his wildly successful "privateering" mission with boundless enthusiasm. He and his crew auctioned plundered calicos, muslin, silk, spices and dyes on the docks without fear of arrest for piracy. According to Johnson, Tew's Bermuda investors realized a return worth fourteen times the value of the *Amity*.

Red Sea Fever

Tew could have retired comfortably in his hometown, but that was not to be. After his crew squandered their treasure, some urged Tew to make another voyage to the Red Sea. Their former captain was easily convinced. By October 1694, only months after his return home, Tew prepared for a second voyage. The promise of great wealth, easy targets and the acceptability of sailing against infidels attracted candidates like sharks to blood. Nathaniel Coddington captured the spirit of the time in an account written several years later:

> *All the vessel's* [sic] *…were bound to Madigaskar*[,] *but some sd* [sic] *they were to go to the Red Seas where the mony* [sic] *was plenty as stones, & sand, saying the people there was* [sic] *Infidels, & it was no sin to kill them. Capt Thomas Tew…(planned) a second Voyage…many was* [sic] *the young men* [who] *went out belonging to this place where some few returned.*[5]

Bogus privateering commissions provided the illusion of legality and attracted investors. Captain Tew and John Bankes asked Newport's governor Easton for commissions. The governor rejected Tew's bribe of £500 because he believed Rhode Island needed seamen for defense against the French.

Tew next sought a commission from New York's governor Fletcher. The dapper mariner was described in Bishop's *The Exotics* as being slight, dark and about forty years old. Elegantly dressed in a blue jacket with gold lace trim, Tew attracted attention as he rode through the city in the governor's six-horse coach. White linen trousers ended at his knees, embroidered stockings covered his legs, a gold chain hung about his neck and a jewel-encrusted dagger hung on his belt.

Governor Fletcher thought highly of Tew and enjoyed hearing his tales of pirate raids. A fee, probably a bribe, of £300 convinced Fletcher to grant Tew a commission to cruise against the French in the Saint Lawrence River. No one expected Tew to cruise against the French.

Tew sailed in the *Amity* to the Red Sea with four consorts, Thomas Wake on the *Susanna* William Want on the *Dolphin* and two Newporters—William Mayes on the *Pearl* and John Bankes on the *Portsmouth Adventure*. Mayes and Bankes received clearances from Robert Gardner, Newport's deputy collector of customs.

American Gentlemen of Fortune Join Captain Avery

In June 1695, Tew and company encountered Captain John "Long Ben" Avery in the Red Sea. Long Ben Avery carved himself a place of distinction in the history of English piracy. King William's general pardon of 1698 excluded only two pirates by name: John Avery and William Kidd.

Thinking there would be strength in numbers, the five Americans gave Avery command of the fleet. The pirates hid near the entrance to the Red Sea for two months waiting for treasure ships to sail from Surat. The lack of prospects caused them to doubt the wisdom of their strategy. That doubt turned to disappointment when they learned, from a captured ketch, that twenty-five Indian vessels sailed past their sleeping ships. The pirates set off in pursuit.

Only the *Portsmouth Adventure* and the *Susanna* kept pace with Avery. The *Dolphin* was so slow that its crew joined Avery's crew and burned the *Dolphin*. They took the *Pearl* in tow. Captain Tew did not keep up. Three days later, the pirates overtook one of the Indian ships. It belonged to the wealthiest

He Had Found the Captain Agreeable and Companionable, an illustration of Captain Thomas Tew and Governor Fletcher. Howard Pyle illustration. *From* Harper's Magazine, *November 1894.*

merchant of Surat. After a skirmish, the freebooters captured it and relieved their prize of £60,000 in silver and gold.

That was a substantial fortune, but it paled next to the one plundered from their next victim. The *Ganj-i-sawai* (*Esteemed Treasure*) belonged to the Great Mogul. A formidable vessel of forty guns, it was the largest ship out of Surat. Avery and his Newport companions encountered it near Bombay. What happened next made the pirates' fortunes and sealed their fate.

One of the Indians' guns burst and killed several of their men. The English shot down the ship's mainmast and, despite being outnumbered, boarded their prize. Days of plunder followed. Women threw themselves into the sea or killed themselves to escape abuse by the marauders. The pirates stole gold, silver, jewels and a ruby-encrusted saddle and bridle intended for the Great Mogul. Everyone but Captain Tew and the crew of the *Amity* was on hand to share the plunder.

News of the attack reached the Great Mogul and his subjects. Rioting crowds made it necessary for the mogul's governor to send guards to protect the East India Company and its English employees. London's East India Company pressured Parliament to put an end to Red Sea pirating. Parliament issued a proclamation against Avery and gave Captains Thomas Tew, Thomas Wake and William Mayes prominent billing in Captain Kidd's 1696 pirate-hunting commission.

Thomas Tew did not live long enough to be hunted. When the *Amity* returned to Madagascar, its captain was not on board. He had been killed during an attack on a ship owned by the Great Mogul.

Thomas Tew enjoyed the pirates' proverbial short but merry life. Thomas Paine, another Newport pirate, avoided that fate.

4

Captain Thomas Paine

Captain Thomas Paine was a Caribbean pirate, friend of Captain Kidd and one of the founders of Trinity Church. He also led Rhode Island in its first naval victory.

Early Years

Thomas Paine sailed the Caribbean with French privateers and pirates, including Captain Peckar. In 1682, Paine convinced Jamaica's governor to grant him a commission to hunt pirates. Since Paine had never harmed an Englishman, a ringing endorsement for an English pirate, Governor Lynch honored the captain's request.

Pirate Captain

Paine commanded a crew of sixty on the *Pearl*, a frigate carrying eight guns. He sailed it into New Providence, the Bahamas. His commission's directive, to hunt pirates, played no role in Paine's subsequent adventures. Paine and his crew decided to dive for silver from a nearby Spanish wreck. He and four other captains organized a "wrecking party," but picking silver off the ocean floor lost its appeal.

Line drawing of a frigate. *Pearson Scott Foresman.*

A new scheme seized their collective imaginations—to attack the Spanish settlement of Saint Augustine on Florida's east coast. Saint Augustine mounted a formidable defense and forced the pirates to retreat. They resorted to plundering small settlements.

Paine and two consorts eventually returned to New Providence with renewed enthusiasm to dive for Spanish silver, but their raids along Florida's coast convinced the Bahamian governor that the pirates belonged in the island's jail. Paine escaped capture. It took a year for his reputation as a pirate to reach London. When it did, in 1684, the king sent letters to the governors of Jamaica and Massachusetts instructing them not to harbor or assist any pirates, particularly not Thomas Paine.

Newport

Paine sailed the *Pearl* into Newport during the summer of 1683, only a few months after his attacks in Florida. While news of those attacks had not yet reached Newport, Paine's arrival attracted a different controversy. Boston suspected that the *Pearl* was an "unfreebottomed ship," a foreign vessel not allowed to trade in the colonies. An early Navigation Act permitted only English ships to trade in English colonies. Boston's deputy collector of customs Thomas Thatcher arrived in Newport to investigate. His suspicions were confirmed.

Thatcher asked Rhode Island governor Coddington to arrest Paine. Coddington informed Thatcher that Paine had produced a privateer's commission from Sir Thomas Lynch, governor of Jamaica. Paine had, no doubt, also produced cold, hard cash.

Coddington disputed evidence that cast doubt on the authenticity of Paine's commission. When Thatcher informed the governor of Paine's attempt on Saint Augustine and attacks on neighboring towns, Coddington told him to take that matter up with the courts. Thatcher returned to Boston.

In Chapin's article, "Captain Paine of Cajacet," he explained that, after the king's letter arrived in Boston, William Dyer, a royal agent, arrested Captain Thomas Paine, arch-pirate. Dyer also charged Governor Coddington with neglect for not seizing Paine and his ship. Paine was eventually released.

Another deputy collector from Boston granted clearance for Captain Paine and the *Pearl* for a fee: one-third of the vessel's estimated value. Captain Paine paid the fee, and his legal problems came to an end. Thomas Paine found a friendly port to begin his new life.

From Pirate to Landlubber

Paine also found a wife, Mercy Carr, the daughter of Justice Caleb Carr, a future Rhode Island governor. The former pirate purchased land and lived quietly as a farmer in Jamestown on nearby Conanicut Island. Paine's roving days were over.

It took a war to bring the old pirate off his farm. Ironically, it was to hunt pirates, exactly what Paine's Jamaican commission expected him to do. During King William's War, three French "privateers" commanded by Captain Peckar, Paine's former Caribbean associate, spent a week raiding

Block Island, Rhode Island. The marauders shot cattle, stole whatever they wanted, beat up some of the inhabitants to get them to reveal where they hid treasure and made unsuccessful advances on Mrs. Rodman, "a very desirable gentlewoman."

Paine must have been in his late fifties by then, old by colonial standards, but he was a veteran sea fighter and had more experience in naval warfare than anyone in the colony. Newport fitted out two sloops, one for Captain Paine and the other for Captain John Godfrey. With Paine in command, they sailed for Block Island. An eyewitness described the battle:

> Our English vessels stretched off to the southward, and soon made a discovery of a small fleet standing eastward. Supposing them to be the French they were in quest of, they tacked and came in as near shore as they could with safety, carrying one anchor to wear and another to seaboard, to prevent the French boarding them on each side at once, and to bring their guns and men all on one side, the better to defend themselves and annoy the enemy. The French…made all the sail they could…When they came, they bore down on the English, and there ensued a very hot seafight for several hours…the great barque foremost, pouring in a broadside with small arms. Ours bravely answered them in the same manner, with their huzzas and shouting. Then followed the larger sloop, the captain whereof was a very violent, resolute fellow. He took a glass of wine to drink…But as he was drinking, a bullet struck him in his neck, with which he instantly fell down dead…Thus they passed by in course, and then tacked and brought their other broadside to bear. In this manner they continued the fight until the night came on and prevented their farther conflict. Our men as valiantly paid them back in their own coin, and bravely repulsed them, and killed several of them…But having found the engagement too hot for them, they hoisted their sails and stood off to sea; and one reason might be this…that their Commodore understood…that it was Captain Paine he had encountered, said, "He would as soon choose to fight the devil as with him."[6]

The old pirate delivered the goods. Paine and Godfrey received a hero's welcome, Rhode Island enjoyed its first naval victory and Thomas Paine's position in the colony was solidified. In seven years, the rover had transformed from pirate to colonial hero. His reputation was secure. He would need it to be.

Captain Thomas Paine's Conanicut Island farmhouse. *Photo by Helene Scola.*

Friend of Captain Kidd

In the summer of 1699, Captain William Kidd sailed into Narragansett Bay to see his friend Thomas Paine. Since Kidd was wanted for piracy, he sailed between Conanicut Island and the sparsely populated mainland to avoid Newport and possible arrest. Kidd anchored off Conanicut's northwest shore. One of his men rowed around the island's north end to Paine's farm on the northeast shore and brought Paine to Kidd's boat. Kidd asked Paine to keep "some things" for him. Paine later alleged that he refused that request on the grounds that his house would be searched.

Captain Paine's house was searched months later. An incriminating letter from William Kidd's wife, Sarah, to Thomas Paine led the authorities to do so. That letter, found in a trunk at the home of Captain Samuel Knott, read, in part: "I would desire you to send me Twenty four ounces of Gold and as for all the rest you have in your custody…I shall desire you to keep in your custody."[7]

Sarah Kidd had Captain Knott take her letter from Boston to Rhode Island. Captain Knott rode from Boston to Bristol, Rhode Island; took the ferry to Aquidneck Island; rode to Newport; took the ferry to Paine's farm; and delivered Sarah's letter. Paine gave Knott eight gold bars weighing a total of twenty-eight ounces. Knott returned to Boston with seven bars weighing twenty-two ounces. He claimed a gold bar fell out of his pocket during the journey.

Richard Coote, the Earl of Bellomont, in Newport to pursue Kidd's case and recover his treasure, informed the London Board of Trade that "Mrs. Kidd's Injunction to Pain [*sic*] to keep a[ll the] rest that was left with him 'till further order, was a plain Indication that there was a good deal of [trea]sure still behind in Pain's [*sic*] custody."[8]

Bellomont ordered Newport governor Cranston and Colonel Sanford to search Paine's house. Nothing was found. Paine voluntarily produced about eighteen ounces of gold, allegedly a gift from Kidd. Bellomont did not believe or trust Paine, but the hero was beyond London's reach. The matter ended.

Trinity Church

Lord Bellomont's dispatch to the board of trade regarding Thomas Paine's connection to William Kidd also contained a petition to assign an Anglican minister to Newport. Thomas Paine, one of sixteen signers, was not the

Paine historical cemetery in Jamestown, Rhode Island. Captain Paine's tombstone is at the far left. *Jamestown Historical Society Collection*.

only petitioner with a dicey reputation. Bellomont thought the presence of an Anglican minister would "be a means, I hope, to reform the lives of the people and make good Christians of 'em, who at present are all in darkness."[9]

A Respectable Citizen

According to Chapin's article, Captain Thomas Paine lived a model life in Rhode Island. He served on a grand jury, was appointed tax assessor for Jamestown and became captain of the Jamestown militia. By 1698, Paine was a freeman of the colony with the right to vote. His father-in-law became governor. Captain Paine was well connected and well respected. He passed away in 1715, at eighty-three years of age.

Paine's life was one of adventure, controversy, intrigue and heroism. A fireside chat with Captain Thomas Paine would have been impossible to resist, but his friend Captain Kidd did not live long enough to reminisce by the fire.

5

Captain William Kidd

Was Captain Kidd a pirate or was he the victim of political intrigue? In 1701, opinion came down on the side of pirate. Opinion today leans toward his having been a political scapegoat.

How It Began

William Kidd was an experienced seaman and respected privateer. His heroic actions during King William's War earned him a reputation for bravery. Kidd's experience and reputation attracted the attention of Richard Coote, Earl of Bellomont. King William directed Bellomont to stamp out pirates harassing merchants in the West Indies and Red Sea. Bellomont wanted William Kidd to command the mission. Kidd, a prosperous gentleman of New York with a wife and daughter, did not find Bellomont's offer attractive. It was a no prey, no pay arrangement. The earl talked Kidd into it by promising a larger share of the take.

Bellomont, four high-powered aristocrats and King William formed a company to sponsor Kidd's expedition. Kidd's job was to bring pirates to justice and collect their treasure. Proceeds from condemned vessels and booty would be divided among the company. The commission did not address the fact that the original owners of pirate plunder had a legal right to compensation:

To our trusty and well beloved Captain William Kid…Whereas we are informed, that Captain Thomas Too [Tew], John Ireland, Captain Thomas Wake, and Captain William Maze…and other Subjects…have associated themselves, with divers others, wicked and ill disposed Persons, and do, against the Law of Nations, commit many and great Pyracies, Robberies and Depredations on the Seas upon the Parts of America, and in other Parts, to the great Hinderance and Discouragement of Trade and Navigation…to bring the said Pyrates, Free Booters and Sea Rovers to Justice…with all their Ships and Vessels; and all such Merchandizes, Money, Goods and Wares as shall be found on board. [10]

Since England was at war with France, an additional Commission of Reprisals gave Kidd authority to privateer against French merchant ships.

Kidd's Ill-Fated Voyage

In *The Pirate Hunter,* Zacks gave a thorough account of Kidd's story. Kidd's ship, the *Adventure Galley*, a powerful privateer with thirty-four guns, needed at least 100 men. Finding a crew in Plymouth, England, proved difficult. Then, a Royal Navy captain pressed Kidd's best recruits into service before Kidd left the Thames. The navy captain replaced them with less desirable sailors. Kidd sailed to New York in 1696 with only 75 men. He managed to gather a total of 155 while anchored in the Hudson. Many were deserters, brawlers and down-on-their-luck seamen who had, no doubt, sailed under the black flag. Respectable mariners preferred to privateer against enemy merchant vessels. Pirates fought to the death, and there was no guarantee that their hold would be full of booty.

Kidd began his cruise hunting pirates in the West Indies. Not finding any, he set sail for the Indian Ocean. Nine months later, the *Adventure Galley* was in sight of Madagascar. Kidd was low on provisions and funds, and his unsavory crew was in a foul mood. Kidd stole enough gold from a wrecked French ship to buy provisions. That dishonorable act was marginally acceptable under the king's commission. A handful of minor piratical raids followed with little gain.

When two Muslim ships fell within reach, Kidd attacked. After looting and burning one, Kidd replaced his *Adventure Galley* with the other. Kidd justified his attack on the basis that both ships carried French commissions. He secured the French passes and became captain of the *Quedah Merchant*, which he renamed the *Adventure Prize*.

Kidd anchored off Madagascar to move from the *Adventure Galley* to the *Adventure Prize*. Robert Culliford, a notorious Red Sea pirate, was in the harbor. Ninety-five members of Kidd's disgruntled crew deserted him to join Culliford. Kidd cut his losses and sailed for home. Over two years after embarking from England, Kidd arrived at Anguilla, a small island in the West Indies. He had little to show for his efforts, but that was the least of his problems.

In Anguilla, Kidd learned he was wanted for piracy and that King Williams's 1698 Act of Grace offered amnesty to all pirates, excluding Captain Avery and himself. Kidd was on the run and anxious to contact Bellomont, but the notorious pirate had to find Bellomont before the authorities found him. Kidd had friends in New York and Rhode Island. He decided to take shelter in Narragansett Bay and sort things out.

Some of Kidd's crew stayed with the *Adventure Prize* and considerable treasure on Hispaniola. Kidd and the rest of his crew loaded the bulk of their booty on a sloop called the *San Antonio*. The *San Antonio* brought Captain Kidd to Narragansett Bay.

Sands family homestead marker in Block Island, Rhode Island. *Photo by Helene Scola.*

Captain Kidd's Block Island Visit

In June 1699, Boston's *Campbell Newsletter* reported that when Captain Kidd arrived in Narragansett Bay, the governor sent thirty well-armed men in a boat out of Newport to seize him. Kidd shot two great guns at the boat, and it retreated. That was the only documented exchange of fire with Kidd. Since Governor Cranston was Kidd's friend, the attack out of Newport may have been strictly for show.

Kidd's wife, Sarah, and their daughter stayed with Mary and Edward Sands on Block Island to wait for his arrival. Kidd anchored the *San Antonio* off the east coast of Block Island, near the Sands' homestead, and sent a boat to shore for Sarah and their daughter.

Kidd arranged to have New York lawyer James Emmott, an old friend, brought to his boat. Emmott agreed to contact Bellomont on Kidd's behalf. Kidd entrusted Emmett with the two French passes to give to the earl. The lawyer was to tell Bellomont that, if he would arrange for a pardon, Kidd would bring his sloop with all its treasure to Boston and retrieve the *Adventure Prize* with the rest of the booty.

Bellomont's appetite for gain conflicted with orders to arrest Kidd and ship him to London. The duplicitous man decided to lure Kidd to Boston with the promise of pardon, arrest him and secure his treasure. Kidd believed Bellomont well enough to go to Boston, but not so well as to take his treasure with him. He sailed west to Gardiner's Island, east of Long Island, and sent for John Gardiner, the owner.

After burying most of his treasure on Gardiner's property, Kidd sailed up Narragansett Bay to visit Thomas Paine and arrange for Mrs. Kidd to receive a portion of his wealth. Paine's deposition, quoted in the October 1885 edition of the *Rhode Island History Magazine*, revealed that Kidd also sent a man to bring Governor Cranston to his boat. Rhode Island legend maintains that Kidd anchored either off Conanicut's shore or in Jamestown's Mackerel Cove to meet with his friend Governor Cranston. Paine's deposition lends credibility to that legend.

An interesting piece of information provided by Tim Cranston, a descendant of Governor Cranston, also supports the legend. Tim has a document dated September 26, 1699, signed by Governor Samuel Cranston, stating that Captain Kidd worked under the governor's direction in Narragansett Bay "last spring." It is possible that, during his visit to Jamestown, Kidd requested the document from Cranston to help him convince London that he was in Newport, not the Red Sea, during the time in question. Samuel Cranston, a fellow Scott, would have been happy to help Kidd win his pardon in England.

Kidd returned to Long Island, settled his affairs with John Gardiner and sailed to Boston. Bellomont's treachery resulted in Kidd's arrest and imprisonment on His Majesty's ship *Active*. Kidd sailed for London in chains.

In *Semper Eadem*, Hattendorf revealed that a Royal Navy chaplain, James Honyman, ministered to Kidd during his voyage to London. Reverend Honyman eventually became minister of Newport's Trinity Church.

Map of New England and New York, detail of Long Island and Block Island, by John Speed, 1676. *Courtesy of Redwood Library & Athenaeum, Newport, Rhode Island.*

How It Ended

The group of aristocrats that sponsored Kidd's expedition included Lord Somers, the lord chancellor. Somers's involvement posed a problem after Kidd's transformation from pirate hunter to hunted pirate was complete. In *The Book of Buried Treasure*, R.D. Paine recounted that, when Kidd arrived in London, a power struggle raged between the Whigs and the Tories. Parliament attempted to impeach Lord Somers. Somers's association with Kidd's ill-fated commission and subsequent arrest for piracy fueled the Tories' case. The lord chancellor wanted nothing to do with his former partner. Neither did the king, Lord Bellomont or any of Kidd's Whig sponsors. They dissolved the company.

In his defense, Kidd accused his men of mutinying against him when he refused to plunder, locking him in his cabin, threatening to kill him, disobeying his order to attack the notorious pirate Culliford, joining Culliford's crew and setting fire to his ship. There was, however, the murder of his mutinous gunner, Mr. Moore, to be explained.

Bellomont captured Joseph Palmer, a member of Kidd's crew, in Newport. Palmer informed Bellomont that Kidd hit Moore on the right side of his head with a bucket bound with iron hoops. Moore died the next day. Palmer's testimony won him his freedom and helped send Kidd to the gallows. It was not unusual for crew members on naval and merchant ships to die as the result of their captain's brutality, but it was unusual for the captain to be charged with murder and executed.

Kidd's trial for piracy began after he was convicted of Moore's murder. Since Kidd could not be executed twice, London pursued his piracy trial to mollify the East India Company and the Great Mogul.

The two French East India Company passes disappeared. Had they been produced, they could have saved Kidd's life. But that might have ended the career of the lord chancellor and complicated the lives of Kidd's sponsors. Kidd was a political liability. He had to disappear and so did the passes. R.D. Paine, author of *The Book of Buried Treasure*, discovered one of those passes in 1910. Kidd had not imagined them after all, which the lord chief baron had claimed.

John Gardiner delivered Kidd's treasure to Bellomont. Officers of the Crown confiscated most of the fortune. Assorted lawyers received their shares. Lord Bellomont did not receive any of Kidd's treasure. He died penniless and in debt two and a half months before Kidd's execution. One positive result came of Kidd's conviction. Zacks explained that, after

View of Block Island Harbor, where Captain Kidd anchored. *Photo by Helene Scola.*

everyone received their portion of his treasure, an act of Parliament arranged to donate £4,000 to Greenwich Hospital for Retired Sailors.

Before Captain Kidd arrived in Narragansett Bay, crew members who deserted him in Madagascar sailed into Newport. While Captain Kidd buried his treasure and negotiated with Bellomont, remnants of Tew's and Avery's crews drifted into Newport. Lord Bellomont had work to do.

6

𝔚𝔦𝔠𝔨𝔢𝔡 𝔞𝔫𝔡 𝔦𝔩𝔩-𝔇𝔦𝔰𝔭𝔬𝔰𝔢𝔡 𝔓𝔢𝔯𝔰𝔬𝔫𝔰

Madagascar was a pirate haven throughout the late seventeenth and early eighteenth centuries. Using Madagascar as a base, English and Anglo-American Red Sea pirates traded or sold stolen goods, purchased supplies and provisions, cleaned and repaired ships, fitted out, enjoyed a little rest and relaxation and embarked on pirate raids. Avery's capture of the Great Mogul's ship and Kidd's apparent piracy convinced Parliament of the need to eliminate the vermin. King William's 1698 Act of Grace was part of that strategy. England pursued Avery and his crew on their side of the Atlantic. London took aim at the heart of pirate patronage by replacing New York's corrupt Governor Fletcher with Lord Bellomont and charging Bellomont with tracking down Kidd and other pirates in the colonies. London was determined to succeed in the wake of Kidd's failure.

Captain John Avery

Newport pirates Tew, Wake and Mayes came to London's attention as a result of Red Sea raids with Captain John Avery (also known as Henry Every and Long Ben Avery). Those raids earned the Newporters top billing on Captain Kidd's pirate-hunting commission.

Captain Avery began his career in the Royal Navy. When he served as second mate on the privateer *Charles*, Avery led a mutiny, became the ship's commander and renamed it *Fancy*. He and his crew plundered south along Africa's west coast. Their goal, the Red Sea, was where the Newport pirates, led by Avery, captured the Great Mogul's ship and roused England's anger.

England never captured Captain Avery. He was rumored to have lived like royalty on a tropical island, but there is evidence that he died penniless in Great Britain. England captured six members of his crew and executed them in 1696.

Adam Baldrich, Madagascar Trader

Adam Baldrich abandoned his life as a Caribbean buccaneer to establish a trading post on Saint Mary's Island off Madagascar's northeast coast. From 1691 to 1697, he provided Red Sea pirates with weapons, gunpowder, ship's provisions, food and drink. They provided Baldrich with gold, silver, silks and slaves. Baldrich sold the pirated goods to New York merchants.

Captain Baldrich's log incriminated Captains Tew, Wake and Mayes in attacks on Red Sea shipping. On October 19, 1693, the *Amity* arrived on Saint Mary's with Tew in command. The crew used treasure taken from a Moorish ship to buy provisions.

Two years later, the *Susanna*, captained by Thomas Wake, arrived at Baldrich's trading post. Captain Wake and most of his men became ill and died on the island. Surviving crew members joined Captain Hore, another pirate with Newport connections.

Jameson included a deposition explaining that Moors killed Captain Tew before the *Amity* returned to Saint Mary's in 1695. His surviving crew sailed the Red Sea until its capture by Moors.

Captain William Mayes

Thomas Tew and Thomas Wake met with King Death in the Indies, but what happened to the third Newport pirate named in Kidd's commission, Captain William Mayes?

William May(s) was one of the six members of Avery's crew tried for piracy in 1696. Some researchers assumed he was William Mayes of Newport. He was not.

London tried William May(s), Joseph Dawson, Ed Forsythe, William Bishop, James Lewis and John Sparks for piracy in 1696. Their acquittal inspired the court to rush through a second indictment on another set of charges. The court accused the group of conspiring with Avery to steal the *Charles* with piratical intent. William May(s) never denied being on the *Charles* but pleaded that he was too ill to take part in the mutiny. That trial resulted in a guilty verdict and the execution of all six pirates. Accounts of both trials can be read in Sollom Emlyn's *A Complete Collection of State Trials.*

Since William May(s) was one of Avery's original crew, he was not William Mayes of Newport. William Mayes was alive, but where?

In 1698, Governor Cranston wrote to the board of trade that "the best information…is, that Capt' Avery and his men plundered him [Mayes]…destroyed him and company, for none…are yet returned."[11]

According to DeFoe, Avery did plunder his Newport consorts. He convinced them to put all the treasure on his larger, faster ship. Several nights later, the *Fancy* slipped anchor and successfully stole all the booty from Tew's former companions, but he did not murder them.

John Dunn, a member of Avery's crew, testified that William Mayes took the *Pearl* to Ethiopia. Mayes could have robbed Muslim ships, sold pirated goods in New York and returned to Madagascar with provisions to sell to Red Sea pirates. Lord Bellomont suggested as much in a letter from New York during the summer of 1699:

> *A great ship has been seen off this Coast…it is supposed to be one Maise [sic], a Pyrate who has brought a vast deale of wealth from the red Seas. There is a Sloop also at Rhoad Island, which is said to be a Pyrate. I hear the men goe a shoar [sic] there in the day time and return to the Sloop at night and spend their gold very liberally.*[12]

London's 1698 replacement of New York's governor Fletcher, pirate patron, with Lord Bellomont, pirate nemesis, changed the game for colonial pirates. Madagascar pirates would have found it expedient to surrender under the 1698 Act of Grace.

Mayes, like Tew, enjoyed a respectable pedigree. William Mayes's grandfather was Samuel Gorton, an early president of Providence and Warwick. His father, William Sr., opened the White Horse Inn in 1682. After William Mayes Sr.'s death, his son would have needed to apply for his own license. A liquor license issued to William Mayes in 1702 suggests that Mayes surrendered under the 1698 Act of Grace and returned to Newport

WHITE HORSE TAVERN
1673
"America's Oldest Tavern"
Yearly Gathering Place of the
Members of the Colonial Legislature

Above: White Horse Tavern in Newport, Rhode Island. *Photo by Helene Scola.*

Left: Historical plaque for the White Horse Tavern in Newport, Rhode Island. *Photo by Helene Scola.*

and the family business. William Mayes Jr. died in 1703. A partial inventory of his estate listed items that a tavern keeper, not a gentleman of fortune, would have possessed. There is no stone to mark the retired pirate's grave, but William Mayes Jr. was probably laid to rest near his father in Newport's Common Burial Ground.

The White Horse Inn became the White Horse Tavern in 1730. It still operates as a restaurant under that name in its original Marlboro Street location.

William Want and John Bankes

John Dunn's deposition, recorded in Jameson, also revealed that Avery met with William Want's *Dolphin* and John Bankes's *Portsmouth Adventure*. Dunn reported that Captain Faro, on Bankes's *Portsmouth Adventure*, brought Avery to Ireland. Bankes, who was not mentioned by Dunn, put Faro in command of his ship. Dunn believed that Want sailed to the Gulf of Persia.

It is safe to assume that Bankes and Want perished in the Indies either during a battle or an ocean storm or fell victim to disease. Nathanial Coddington's account at the time made it clear that few men returned from Tew's second voyage.

Thomas Jones, William Downs, Richard Cornish and Peter Brock

Some of Avery's crew and members of Tew's second voyage returned to Newport. In *Off Soundings*, Hawes revealed how easily Newport absorbed its wayward sons.

Thomas Jones sailed with Avery on the *Fancy*. He arrived home in 1696 and married the daughter of Thomas Townsend, Newport sheriff. William Downs, Thomas Jones's mate on the *Fancy*, was arrested in 1698. Downs walked out of Newport's jail and disappeared. Richard Cornish left with Bankes on the *Portsmouth Adventure* but joined Avery's crew. After his return to Newport, he was tried for piracy. Cornish's tearful testimony convinced the jury that he was only a passenger on Avery's ship. Peter Brock sailed on Bankes's *Portsmouth Adventure*. He became a Newport constable.

7

Red Sea Pirates Wash Ashore

Two weeks before the notorious pirate Captain Kidd anchored off Block Island, Captain Giles Shelley arrived at Cape May, New Jersey, on the *Nassau*. He sailed from Madagascar with about forty pirates as passengers. Some members of Kidd's old crew, those who deserted him for Culliford, sailed on the *Nassau*. With their New York patron, Governor Fletcher, out of office and Lord Bellomont in his place, the market for pirated goods had dried up. Pirates wanted out of Madagascar and to escape the hangman's noose. The chase was on.

About fourteen pirates disembarked at Cape May. New Jersey's governor Basse captured six of them. Despite the evidence of treasure and incriminating information, Basse released all the prisoners, but he did not release their treasure.

Sion Arnold

A Newport man, Sion Arnold, was among those arrested and then freed in New Jersey. Lord Bellomont complained of Arnold's release to the board of trade. Bellomont's avarice was thinly veiled: "Sion Arnold, one of the [pirat]es brought from Madagascar by Shelley of New York…he (Governor Basse) took several Pirates at…Jerzey [*sic*], and a good store of money with them…who can witness what money he seized with them?"[13]

The Old Stone Mill, Newport, RI, attributed to Gilbert Stuart. Gift of Julie Gilmour Bowen. *Courtesy of the Redwood Library & Athenaeum, Newport, Rhode Island.*

Sion's grandfather, Benedict Arnold, served ten terms as governor of Rhode Island. A later Benedict Arnold, the governor's great-grandson, sullied the family name. He became an English spy and traitor during the American Revolution.

Touro Park, on Bellevue Avenue, was part of the Arnold family's extensive farm. A Newport landmark, the ruins of the Viking Tower, also called the Old Stone Mill, is in the park. Several blocks west, on Pelham Street, is the historic Arnold family cemetery.

Lord Bellomont appointed two of Arnold's uncles to a commission charged with collecting evidence of Rhode Island's dealings with pirates. One of the commissioners, Peleg Sanford, questioned Arnold about his relationship to the Red Sea pirate James Gillam. Sanford was not concerned about the young man's acquaintance with Gillam and sent Arnold on his way.

Arnold's adventures in Madagascar cured him of any desire to continue pirating. He had no further scrapes with the law and became a property owner and a freeman of the colony. Arnold eventually inherited a farm in Jamestown, where he lived out the rest of his life.

Joseph Palmer

Joseph Palmer sailed with Arnold on the *Nassau*. He signed onto Kidd's *Adventure Galley* in Plymouth, England, and then deserted him in Madagascar to join the pirate Culliford.

Palmer sailed from New Jersey to Newport, where he was jailed, and released on bail by Governor Cranston. That infuriated Bellomont, in Newport to investigate Kidd. The earl complained to the board of trade: "When I was at Rhode Island, there was one Palmer a Pyrat who was out on bail, for they cannot be persuaded to keep a Pyrat there in Gaol: they love em too well."[14]

Bellomont arrested Palmer, sent him to Boston and interrogated him. During Palmer's interrogation, Bellomont learned about Kidd's fatal attack on his gunner.

Where Everybody Knows Your Name

Thomas Mallett ran an inn out of his Newport home on Clarke Street. He was also a Newport sheriff. Mallett managed to separate the duties of both occupations. In 1699, a suspected pirate, an acquitted pirate and a wanted pirate drank to one another's health in Sheriff Mallett's inn.

Sion Arnold was the suspected pirate, Richard Cornish was the acquitted pirate and James Gillam was the wanted pirate.

James Gillam

A trail of murder, mutiny and piracy preceded Gillam's arrival at Mallett's inn. He pirated in the Indies for years, was captured by natives, escaped and reached Bombay. In 1696, an East India Company ship, the *Mocha*, recruited Gillam and others to replace deserters. It was a fatal mistake.

Gillam led the *Mocha*'s crew in mutiny and murdered its captain. He took command of the ship, renamed it *Resolution* and resumed his piratical career. The pirate captain eventually sailed with Robert Culliford. When most of Kidd's crew joined Culliford, Gillam packed up his treasure and hitched a ride with Captain Kidd to Block Island.

According to Zacks, Mary Sands met Gillam when she visited the *San Antonio* with her friend Sarah Kidd. Mary described Gillam as being about fifty years old, scarred and having dark, leathery skin. Gillam told Mary that he planned to go to Newport. That would not be his first visit. In 1690, Robert Culliford sailed into Newport Harbor on his way to the Red Sea to pick up fellow pirate Gillam.

Gillam assured Mary that Robert Gardner, Newport's deputy collector of customs, promised the colony would provide safe haven to a gentleman of fortune, such as himself. The deputy collector brought Gillam to meet Governor Cranston. Gillam told Cranston that he was not a member of Kidd's crew. Governor Cranston saw no reason to probe further and did not detain him.

Gillam entrusted Thomas Paine with eight hundred pieces of eight and Robert Gardner with gold and silver for safekeeping. In those prebanking days, entrusting valuables to associates was common practice. Robert Gardner furnished Gillam with a "let pass," allowing him to travel from Newport to John Gardiner's Island to retrieve jewels.

In mid-August, Gillam sailed to Block Island with Edward Sands, Mary's husband. By then, word of Gillam's piratical past and the long arm of Lord Bellomont reached Newport. The earl interrogated both Governor Cranston and Robert Gardner. Gillam learned there was a warrant for his arrest and was advised not to remain on Block Island, where his friends could not protect him. Gillam wanted to be taken to Captain Paine's farm, but Sands refused. Gillam stole a small boat—he was a pirate after all—and sailed to Newport.

Gillam arrived in Newport a few weeks after Bellomont questioned Governor Cranston and Deputy Collector Gardner. Bellomont later complained to the board of trade about both Cranston and Gardner. Again, Bellomont's concern for pirate treasure was front and center:

> *An Inventory of gold and Jew*[els] *in Governor Cranston's hands which he took from a Pyrat. I see no reason why he should keep them…he…ought to be called to an account for Conniving at the Py*[rats] *making that Island their Sanctuary, and suffering some to escape from Justice.*[15]
>
> *…Gardiner the Deputy Collector is accused to have been once a Pyrat, in one of the* [paper]*s. I doubt he will forswear himself rather than part with Gillam's gold which is in his hands.* [It is] *impossible for me to transmit to the Lords of the Treasury these proofs against Gardiner.*[16]

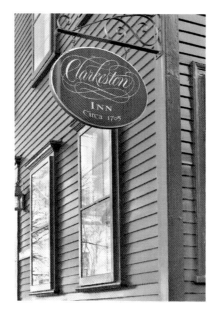

The Clarkeston Inn at 28 Clarke Street in Newport, Rhode Island. Thomas Mallett's Inn was at or near this location. *Photo by Helene Scola.*

Bellomont also questioned Richard Cornish, the acquitted pirate. Cornish stated that he met Gillam at Thomas Mallett's inn. Cornish reported that he said to Gillam, "I see you are not drowned yet." Gillam replied, "Nor you hanged yet."[17]

Sion Arnold was at Mallett's inn that day. He, Cornish and Gillam toasted one another's health. Arnold left with Gillam. Cornish visited Mrs. Mallett in the kitchen. She asked Cornish if Gillam was the wanted pirate. Mrs. Mallett did not get a straight answer.

Gillam left Rhode Island for Boston in late October. He stayed several nights with Andrew Knott, Kidd's friend. Bellomont caught up with Gillam near the house of another pirate, Francis Dowell.

It was a productive night for Bellomont. He arrested both Dowell and Gillam. They sailed with Kidd to their trials and executions in London.

8

A Nest of Pirates

A privateer brought a French vessel into Newport Harbor in 1694. That arrival set two things in motion: the revival of Rhode Island's admiralty court and the privateer captain's transformation into pirate.

Court of Admiralty, Take 2

Rhode Island's admiralty court died of natural causes after the first Dutch war. Interest in its resurrection gained traction when a substantial French prize came into Newport Harbor for condemnation during King William's War.

There was no clause in Rhode Island's charter that allowed a maritime tribunal, but members of the now united colonial assembly, which met in Newport, the colony's capital, believed the colony had a right to set up a court of admiralty should the need arise. When the French prize showed up, the assembly and the governor maintained that, since England was at war, the colony could create an admiralty court.

Appleton's article "Rhode Island's First Court of Admiralty" explained that, in 1694, Rhode Island's legislature passed a law authorizing the governor and his council to act as a court of admiralty. The governor, deputy governor and their assistants presided. Its function was to condemn prizes as necessary. It was wise to encourage privateering against the enemy. Fattening the colony's purse with proceeds from the sale of enemy prizes and their cargo was, no doubt, an afterthought.

John Hore

Captain John Hore had a privateering commission from Jamaica. He captured his French prize, the *St. Paul*, near the Saint Lawrence River. Newport's newly organized admiralty court condemned the ship and its valuable cargo.

Hore took command of the *St. Paul* and renamed it *John and Rebecca*. He applied to Governor Fletcher of New York, Tew's friend and pirate patron, for a commission to cruise against the French. It was no secret that his true objective was the Red Sea. Hore received his bogus privateering commission in 1695 and sailed out of Newport.

According to Baldrich's log, the surviving members of Tew's company on Wake's *Susanna* joined Hore's crew in Madagascar. Hore captured, plundered and burned two Indian ships in August 1696. About six months later, the *John and Rebecca* returned to St. Mary's with another captured ship.

In 1697, Adam Baldrich decided to leave Madagascar. He invited some of the island's natives to a bon voyage party on his boat. Once on board, Baldrich took them prisoner, sailed away and sold them into slavery. That betrayal incited the remaining natives to slaughter the English. Baldrich stated that the natives killed Hore and many of his crew. He never mentioned the reason behind the uprising: "About 8 or 10 days after I [Baldrich] went from St. Maries the Negros killed almost 30 White men upon Madagascar and St. Maries, and took all that they or I had…Captain Hors [*sic*] Ship and Company being all there at the same time."[18]

Hore's surviving crew haunted Lord Bellomont. In 1699, the exasperated earl referred to Hore in a letter condemning Rhode Island's welcoming attitude toward pirates: "John Carr…in Rhode Island…was one of Hore's Crew. There are abundance of other Pyrats in that [Island] and at this time, but they are out of my power."[19]

John Carr, the object of Lord Bellomont's complaint, was a member of Newport's Carr family. The Carrs owned much of what is now Queen Anne's Square. They donated land for the original Trinity Church. Trinity's churchyard occupies that site today. Like so many Newport families, the Carrs were a mix of upstanding citizens, land owners,

Queen Anne's Square with Trinity Church in the background. *Photo by Helene Scola.*

freemen, political leaders and the occasional pirate. John was neither the first nor the only family member to take up piracy. It will be remembered that Captain Thomas Paine, pirate-turned-farmer and friend of Captain Kidd, married Mercy Carr.

Lord Bellomont was sailing hard against the wind.

Robert Glover

Robert Glover, Hore's brother-in-law, fitted out the *Resolution* in Rhode Island, the colonial name for Aquidneck Island, and sailed from Newport to New York, where Governor Fletcher provided him with a privateering commission. On December 29, 1695, the *Resolution* was at St. Mary's. Baldrich revealed that Glover's crew turned him and twenty-four men out of the *Resolution* because they refused to go a-privateering, a euphemism for piracy, in the East Indies. Baldrich boarded the group at his house until they could book passage for Newport.

It sounded like Glover abandoned his roving ways, but it was more likely that the crew's loyalty split, a new captain was elected and Glover was put ashore with men loyal to him. That theory is borne out by the fact that Henry Watson, a prisoner on Hore's ship in 1696, reported that Glover cruised the Gulf of Mocha on a vessel fitted out in Rhode Island.

Evidence placed Glover on St. Mary's during the native uprising: "The Island St. Maries is…well inhabited by black people, where one Captain Baldridge…had built a platform of a Fort with 22 Guns, which was destroyed, together with Captain Glover and the rest of the Pyrats there…by the Blacks."[20]

Glover referred to himself as a mariner out of Antigua. He bequeathed all his silver and gold to his two sons. Glover's sons received their inheritance just months after his will was filed.

Governor Cranston's First Term

Rhode Island enacted a proclamation against piracy in 1698. It read, in part:

> *For the preventing of such evill* [sic] *practices, we his Majesty's Generall Assembly…sitting in Newport…require that all Magistrates and Ministers of Justice…do their utmost endeavor for apprehending such suspected pirates that they may be brought forth to condign punishment: and also to prohibit all persons within this said Collony* [sic] *from entertaining…the said suspected pirates or their goods; but on the contrary, they are strictly required forthwith, upon discovery of any the said persons or goods, to give notice…to some person in authority, and upon neglect…they shall be proceeded against as abettors and confederates with them.*[21]

During the trial of Avery's crew, Rhode Island was accused of being a pirate haven. In a letter to London's Board of Trade, newly elected governor Cranston defended the colony, referred to the recently passed proclamation and further related that "we have seized two persons and their moneys…one Robert Munday, and George Cutler…we shall endeavor to search out the truth, and bring them to a trial."[22]

Robert Munday and George Cutler

In 1698, eight pirates sailed to Newport from Madagascar. They carried enough gold, precious gems, money and East India goods to attract unwelcome attention. Two remained in Newport. Hawes gave an account of their story.

The authorities arrested one of the two, Robert Munday, at the home of Captain Robert Withington and seized all his money. Munday explained that most of it belonged to George Cutler. Cutler arrived several days later and was promptly jailed with Munday. Bail was posted by an uncle of Rhode Island's recently retired governor, Walter Clarke.

Governor Cranston secured the pirates' fortune and planned to appoint a court to try them. If no evidence in support of the charges was presented, they would be released. The trial was to be held in ten months. Meanwhile, Cutler and Munday wandered freely through Newport. Complaints against the pair landed them back in jail. Munday escaped and skipped town before the trial. The law caught up with him four years later. Proof of Munday's piratical activity was available in England. Henry Watson, Hore's prisoner, said Munday was Hore's surgeon's

Wanton-Lyman-Hazard House, built circa 1697, is on the left and the Colony House, 1741, is on the right. The Newport Historical Society offers tours of both colonial sites. *Photo by Helene Scola.*

mate. Apparently that information was not available in Newport because Munday was acquitted. Newport never returned his fortune. It had been forfeited to the colony four years earlier to be used as Governor Cranston saw fit. The colony spent Munday's treasure.

Cutler appeared before Newport's court of general trials in March 1699. He testified that he was left on Madagascar with Captain Glover by the *Resolution*'s crew. That placed him in the group that boarded with Baldrich. Cutler claimed he received some of his money on the Guinea coast and inherited the rest from Mr. Hambleton of Madagascar. Both Cutler and Hambleton sailed on the *Resolution* with Captain Glover during his pirate raids, but no proof in support of the charge of piracy was presented. The court freed Cutler and returned his money.

Cutler bought property, helped fund and found Trinity Church and married the daughter of Governor Arnold.

Joseph Bradish

Two men appeared in Newport to buy a sloop in April 1699. They came from the *Adventure* anchored near Block Island. The ship's crew stole the *Adventure* off Sumatra, elected Joseph Bradish captain and divided its treasure. The pirates buried most of their loot on Long Island.

Newport arrested the men who came ashore and sent two sloops to capture the *Adventure*. When the Newport sloops caught up with him, Bradish and his crew apparently turned on the charm because all three crews got along famously. Bradish invited the Newporters to share the booty. A deal was struck. The Newporters agreed to sell the pirates one of their sloops and allowed them to charter the other. The pirates sank the *Adventure*, and both sloops returned to Newport. Bradish left town.

Boston arrested Bradish and a one-eyed man named Tee Wetherly. The jailer was related to Bradish, so their incarceration was brief. Lord Bellomont vented his frustration in a letter to the board of trade: "That Bradish the Pyrate and one of his Crew were escaped out of the goal [*sic*] of this Town. We have since found that the Goaler [*sic*] was Bradish's kinsman, and the Goaler [*sic*] confessed they went out at the prison door, and that he found it wide open."[23]

Governor Bellomont dismissed the jailer and put the high sheriff in charge. Kidd was held in the same jail a few months later, and Bellomont feared that a "gift" from Kidd would open the cell door. The earl had to pay the new jailer well to keep him honest.

A reward of two hundred pieces of eight for Bradish and one hundred for Wetherly netted the pair. Hawes reported that they joined Kidd in Boston's jail and on his voyage to London to be tried and hanged.

Lord Bellomont vs. the Colony of Rhode Island

While Lord Bellomont was in Rhode Island chasing down Kidd, treasure and assorted pirates, he also investigated the "disorders and irregularities" of the colony. In November 1699, Bellomont sent twenty-five paragraphs of complaints to London. Paragraph number nineteen concerned the colony's relation to pirates and the sham of its proclamation against piracy:

> *The government is notoriously faulty in countenancing and harboring pirates who have openly brought in and disposed of their effects there; whereby the place has been greatly enriched. And not only plain breaches of the Acts of Trade and Navigation have been connived at, but also manifest and known piracies, and all that had been done by them on pretence of seizing and taking up of known pirates has been so slender, weak and not pursued to effect, as plainly demonstrates it was more in show, than out of any hearty zeal or desire to suppress and bring such notorious criminals to Justice, and their care has been so little therein that when they had some of the greatest of those villains in their power, they have suffered them to escape.*[24]

Lord Bellomont, the royal governor of New York, Massachusetts and New Hampshire, lobbied to have Rhode Island's charter revoked. Bellomont wanted Governor Cranston to go the way of Governor Fletcher and to have himself appointed governor of Rhode Island. The earl's death in 1701 probably saved the colony from that fate. Governor Cranston went on to serve twenty-nine terms, more terms than any governor of Rhode Island.

9

Newport's Last Pirate Captain

After an ocean storm separated Captain Black Sam Bellamy on the *Whydah* from Paulsgrave Williams, his pirate consort, Bellamy sailed to Provincetown, Massachusetts, at the north end of Cape Cod. On their way to Provincetown, the pirates captured another ship, *Mary Anne.*

Fog overtook the *Whydah* and the *Mary Anne* along Cape Cod's Atlantic coast. They groped their way north along the treacherous shore. The *Whydah*, a one-hundred-foot galley, sat heavy in the water. Its decks supported twenty-eight cannons and its hold contained 180 fifty-pound bales of treasure looted from more than fifty ships.

Gale-force winds and pounding rain turned a treacherous journey into a deadly one. Thunder rattled the crews' nerves. Forked lightning shredded the black sky. High above the *Whydah*'s pitching deck, the barefoot crew fought the wind and rain to climb rigging, straddle yards and drop sails. Men clung to the bowsprit to secure two spritsails. Each dive of the *Whydah*'s bow plunged them into the boiling sea. Thirty- to forty-foot waves crashed over crew members on deck. They dodged loose cannonballs to secure sails and rigging.

Relentless wind and ocean surf drove the *Whydah* toward shore. In an effort to slow down the ship's progress, Captain Bellamy ordered his crew to drop the *Whydah*'s half-ton anchors. When it was clear that the *Whydah* would run aground, Bellamy had the anchors cut free in an effort to turn the ship's bow toward shore. If he had succeeded, some of his crew might have been able to swim to safety, but the bow turned toward the ocean. Thirty-foot-high waves beat against the helpless *Whydah*.

Map of New England and New York, detail of Block Island to Cape Cod, by John Speed, 1676. *Courtesy of Redwood Library & Athenaeum, Newport, Rhode Island.*

Powerful waves broke the *Whydah*'s cannons free of their mounts. They slammed across the deck, crushing everything in their path, including men. Heavy bales and chests stored in the hold smashed into the *Whydah*'s hull. The roaring ocean swamped the ship's decks. When all three of the *Whydah*'s masts snapped, the ship's crew tried to hack through the rigging with axes to free them and toss them overboard. It was an impossible job under brutal conditions. Ocean waves swept crew and cannon into the sea.

Just past midnight, the *Whydah*'s stern drove into a sandbar. The ship split in half, capsized and sank. Over one hundred bodies washed ashore that night. Some of the *Whydah*'s treasure washed ashore as well. Local wreckers (scavengers) showed up in force, but most of the pirates' fortune was lost with the *Whydah*.[25]

Twenty-eight-year-old Captain Bellamy's piratical career ended with his death that April night in 1717. Captain Paulsgrave Williams's piratical career continued. Williams, a Newporter, was on Block Island visiting family when his partner sailed to Cape Cod. A favorable wind and a touch of homesickness combined to save Williams's life.

Paulsgrave (Paul) Williams

Williams's partnership with Bellamy began in 1716. Clifford wrote a comprehensive account of their story in *Expedition Whydah*. The two men met and drank together at the Great Island Tavern in Provincetown. Israel Cole, a smuggler, built the tavern. It was a popular watering hole and outlet for smuggled and pirated goods.

Paulsgrave Williams was descended from Hew Williams, one of Block Island's original settlers. His father, John, was a Newport merchant and freeman of the colony and served as Rhode Island's Attorney General. Paulsgrave, also a freeman of Newport, supported his wife, son and daughter as a jeweler.

When word that a Spanish treasure fleet sank off Florida's coast reached Provincetown, Sam Bellamy, an English mariner, caught "treasure-fever." Williams contracted the "disease" during his visit. Dreams of Spanish gold lured Williams from domestic life and his Newport business. He decided to purchase a small sloop with Bellamy. The partners rounded up a crew of twelve. Bellamy captained the sloop; Williams was quartermaster. They sailed for Florida to salvage treasure.

After their arrival, Bellamy and Williams learned that Spain had secured the area. They abandoned their plan to retrieve Spanish loot. The adventurers could either return to Provincetown with nothing to show for their efforts or try their hand at pirating. Prosperous Caribbean shipping tempted the crew into going on the account.

They met up with two veteran sea-robbers, Captain Benjamin Hornygold and Captain Louis Lebous. Hornygold's most notorious protégé was the pirate Blackbeard. Bellamy and Williams fell into capable hands. The partnership thrived. Their plunder and crew expanded, but a problem arose when Hornygold and twenty-six men chose not to attack English vessels, including those of English colonists. Williams and Bellamy did not share Hornygold's scruples. Hornygold and his crew sailed off in one sloop. Bellamy was elected captain of the other sloop.

Bellamy and Williams took numerous prizes in the Caribbean. One capture added a flagship. Bellamy took it over, and Williams became captain of the sloop.

In February 1717, the *Whydah*, a three-hundred-ton slaver, was on its way back to London. It carried elephant tusks, gold dust, sugar, indigo and other goods traded for slaves. Bellamy and Williams caught up with the ship between Cuba and Puerto Rico. It surrendered with little resistance. The capture of the *Whydah* placed Bellamy first on *Forbes* magazine's list of "Top-Earning Pirates." *Forbes* estimated his wealth at $120 million.

Bellamy chose the *Whydah* as his new flagship. The pirates rewarded the ship's former master, Captain Prince, for his easy surrender. They gave him one of their ships and permitted Prince and most of his crew to sail away.

Bellamy and Williams sailed their two ships north along the Atlantic coast. Their journey went well until a thunderstorm blew out of the northwest and drove them into the Atlantic Ocean. The wind and sea battered Williams's sloop and Bellamy's ship for four days. When the weather cleared, the wind came in from the south. The pirates rode it north to Rhode Island.

On the way, they captured a Boston sloop commanded by Captain Beer from Newport. The pirates plundered and sank their prize. Despite Sam Bellamy's best efforts, Captain Beer refused to join his crew. Williams later put Beer ashore on Block Island. It would have been bad form for a Newport pirate to hold a Newport captain against his will.

When another storm threatened to separate the pirates, they agreed to meet in Maine. Williams arrived safely on Block Island, but Bellamy was blown east, past Nantucket Shoals.

Bellamy decided to stop in Provincetown before sailing to Maine. He sailed north along the coast of Cape Cod into the jaws of the April storm that claimed most of the pirates' lives.

A *Boston Newsletter* article of May 3, 1717 reported the story:

> *On Monday last arrived here* [Newport] *one Capt. Beer from Block Island, who belongs to this Place…was taken by a Pyrate Sloop and 40 men, commanded by one Paul Williams Captain and Richard Cavily, Master, both of this Island. This Capt. Williams has a Consort, she is call'd the Whido* [sic], *Samuel Bellame Commander…Capt. Williams*

Block Island Historical Society Museum. The museum's engaging collection includes a map showing where Paulsgrave Williams's family lived. *Photo by Helene Scola.*

was for giving Beer his Sloop…but the Ship's Crew ordered her to be sunk; so Williams put him on shore at Block Island; and we are told, that the said Ship is cast away at Cape Cod, and 30 of her Crew drown'd.

Considerably more than thirty of the ship's crew drowned. Boston freed two pirates known to have survived the *Whydah*: John Julian and Thomas Davis. Julian, a Native American from Cape Cod, was never tried. Davis convinced the court that he was a forced man. Seven pirates survived the *Mary Anne*. The authorities arrested them on shore. A Boston court found six of them guilty and executed them.

Some of the *Whydah*'s crew survived and escaped justice. Pirates captured Daniel Collins's Cape Ann fishing sloop on May 10, 1717. Collins said the nineteen pirates told him they escaped the *Whydah* in a longboat. The survivors claimed they had also taken four Marblehead boats.[26]

Williams sailed to the scene as soon as he learned about Bellamy's wreck, but there was nothing he could do. His pirate brethren and all their plunder were lost. After leaving Cape Cod, Williams sailed south and attacked two boats in Vineyard Sound. Two sloops set out from Newport to search for Williams, but they never found him.

A May 10 *Boston Newsletter* article reported Williams's activity: "On Wednesday last our [Newport] Government fitted out two good Sloops, well Arm'd and Man'd, under the command of Col. John Cranston, and Captain Job Almy, in order to speak with a Pirate Sloop lurking on our Coast, commanded by Paul Williams." (Colonel John Cranston was Governor Samuel Cranston's brother.) Williams attacked a vessel off New York in June. He took provisions and forced a carpenter to join the crew.

Old Stone Mill at Newport, artist unknown. *Courtesy of the Redwood Library & Athenaeum, Newport, Rhode Island.*

Williams eventually released the carpenter, but New York jailed two crew members accidently left behind.

Williams's subsequent pirating netted supplies, rigging, lines, sails, provisions and wine. The *Boston Newsletter* reported Williams's final captures in June 1717: "Brown in a Sloop from South Carolina, who was taken on the 14th…by Paul Williams the Pirate, who took from him 350 Ounces of Silver, which was buried in his Ballast, for hiding it: The Pirates threaten'd to burn his sloop…The Pirates Barbarously beat Radford…bound for Surranam."

Williams surrendered under the September 5, 1717 Act of Grace. The retired sea-robber reputedly managed a pirate supply base in the Bahamas.

Paulsgrave Williams was the last Newport seaman to become a pirate captain. By the time he and Bellamy sailed, the sun was setting on piracy's golden age. An act of Parliament passed in 1700 helped to hasten its end. That legislation allowed English colonies to convene vice-admiralty courts. Pirates who preyed on colonial shipping could be arrested, tried and executed where they committed their crimes. Newport was no longer a safe haven.

10
𝕸𝖚𝖉𝖉𝖞 𝖂𝖆𝖙𝖊𝖗𝖘

R hode Island had a responsibility to protect Newport mariners like
Captain Beer, but the colony had a soft spot for local pirates who
did not interfere with local shipping. One murky case demonstrated
Newport's dilemma.

Victim or Pirate?

Bartholomew Roberts, the notorious English pirate, captured a Newport
brigantine in the West Indies in 1721. The ship's captain, Benjamin Norton,
and his crew sailed with Roberts for weeks, presumably as prisoners.

During that time, Roberts captured a Dutch ship loaded with sugar, cocoa
and slaves. He traded that prize and its contents for Norton's less valuable
brigantine. That questionable trade and Norton's subsequent behavior gave
rise to accusations of piracy.

In order to avoid both attention and taxes, Norton sailed the Dutch vessel
into Tarpaulin Cove, north of Martha's Vineyard Island. He contacted the
owner of his brigantine, Newport merchant Joseph Whipple, to give him the
good news. Whipple sent sloops and small traders to offload the cargo and
deliver it to his brother, Captain John Whipple.

In May 1721, the *Boston Newsletter* ran a brief notice: "The large Ship that
Benjamin Norton the Pirate, came in from the West Indies to Tarpaulin

Cove, was seized…after he and his Men had Deserted her, is now brought in here [Boston] with the remaining part of her Cargo, that he and his men had not carried away in Sloops."

Benjamin Norton visited Governor Cranston to explain that Roberts forced one of his seamen to join the pirates and protested his innocence. The governor understood and convinced the *Boston Newsletter* to retract their statement that Norton was a pirate.

Customs officers from Massachusetts and Rhode Island seized the Dutch ship. The fact that most of its cargo slipped out of their hands angered the authorities. Admiralty court judge John Menzies complained to the secretary of the admiralty in Massachusetts:

> *One Benjamin Norton of Rhode-Island, and one Joseph Whippole, a Considerable Merchant of that Colony, did fit out a Brigantine, and sent her under the Command of said Norton to the West Indies…who Fell in with the Pirates…and was (as he saith) taken by One Roberts a Pirate, though…it appears, he is more to be considered as one of their Assistants and Correspondents, for after he had remained with them Six or Seven Weeks, They took a Ship Dutch…and having Loaded her with Sugars, Cocoa, Negroes, etc. of very considerable Value, All this they gave to him for his Brigantine, though of much more Value than She…[Norton] comes with this Ship and Cargo into Tarpaulin Cove…he fired at, and brought too several of Our Coasters.*[27]

Menzies's complaint continued regarding his visit to Newport to fulfill his obligation to "secure the goods of all pirates." Rhode Island's governor Cranston stonewalled him:

> *That the Governor considers himself as Vice Admiral and that as such he hath right to intromett with All Goods belonging to Pirates…and that he would not allow me with the Priviledge of the Court House, unless I would comply with and acquiesce in their Acts of Council. To which I replyed, Their Charter contains no such Grant of Admiralty jurisdiction nor right to any Piratical Goods…[they] not only Debarred me from the Use of the Court House but also to deliver up the Negroes.*[28]

Menzies pointed out that the "Negroes" were "sold amongst themselves at an undervalue." A *Boston Newsletter* article in June 1721 referred to a court of admiralty sale in Newport. The goods sound like those from Norton's ship:

Horse trough fountain at Washington Square was the site of Newport's Town School House and an 1721 admiralty court auction. *Photo by Helene Scola.*

> *By Order of the Court of Admiralty, There are Nineteen Negroes whereof Two are Men, Eleven Women, Four Boyes & Two Girls, to be Exposed to Sale...at the Town School House of said New Port. As also...Sale by Order of said Court, Twenty seven Bags of Cocoa, and seven Hogsheads of Sugar at the same place.*

Newport's Town School House, the site of the auction, was on the Parade, today's George Washington Square. The horse trough fountain is on or near the school's eighteenth-century location.

Selling the slaves for less than they were worth irritated Menzies, but the fact that Newport sold them by order of the court of admiralty profoundly upset the duly appointed admiralty court judge. Boston did not recognize Rhode Island's authority to convene a court of admiralty or its right to pirate loot. Profiting from pirated goods was equally as important as apprehending the rogues. Everyone wanted his share.

Two years after the sale of Norton's cargo, John Menzies published a Court of Admiralty Act and Order in the *Boston Gazette*:

Act and Order, by John Menzies Esq; Judge of Vice-Admiralty in the Province of Massachusetts-Bay and New-Hampshire, Colony of Rhode-Island, Providence Plantation, and Narraganset Country in New-England in America.

WHEARAS the Ship El-Puerto-Delprincipe, *brought in by Benjamin Norton to Tarpolin-Cove, Anno 1721, and which had been Piratically improved, was Seized and Condemned with her Cargo, in the Court of Admiralty, and the Produce remains as yet in the Hands of sundry Persons…the whole Produce thereof to be delivered into and remain in the hand of the Judge of Vice-Admiralty in New England…It is…hereby Ordained that all Persons who have any parts of the produce of the said Ship and Cargo in their hands…pay and deliver up the same to the Judge of Vice Admiralty in New England…if they…do not comply…they will be then Prosecuted for recovery thereof in such manner as the Law will admit.*

The order's introductory line stated that Menzies was the judge of the vice-admiralty for the colony of Rhode Island, an unmistakable slap across Governor Cranston's face. Menzies avoided calling Norton a pirate but noted that his ship "had been Piratically improved." According to Pringle in *Jolly Roger*, piratical improvements included raised gunwales and decks cleared of structures that would impede traffic during battle. Removing deck structures also reduced the vessel's weight and increased its speed. Its hold would have been opened up to allow free access, as well. Contemporary readers understood Menzies's implications.

Menzies wanted everything from Norton's ship that was sold in Newport delivered to him. He had a long memory and an arm long enough to reach Newport from Boston.

A postscript to Norton's encounter with Bartholomew Roberts appeared in the *Boston Gazette* the same year that Menzies's Vice-Admiralty Court Order was published: "We have Advice from Antigua, that Capt. John Finny, his Gunner and 3 Men that did belong to Norton's Brigt. & were left at Tobago, were hanged there. And they there heard that the Hector Man of War hath taken the rest of the Pirates that were left at Tobago."

Norton was a Newporter. Whether he was a pirate or a victim is unclear—maybe he was both. But because he was a homeboy, it was OK.

As Rhode Island's merchant fleet grew, pirates captured more Newport mariners. Something had to be done.

11

The Tide Turned

From the late 1600s to the early 1700s, Newport had more to gain than to lose by welcoming pirates. Their activity provided both employment and profit. Cash-starved colonists welcomed foreign gold and silver. They also welcomed cut-rate prices for luxury goods. Plus, neither the currency nor the ill-gotten gains came at the expense of local merchants or investors.

The end of Queen Anne's War in 1714 changed everything. In *Between the Devil and the Deep Blue Sea*, Rediker explained that, during the war, the Royal Navy employed 49,860 men. By war's end, that number had dropped to 13,475. Privateering commissions expired, terminating the employment of many more sailors. Fewer jobs meant a surplus of labor and lower wages. Sailors had to either "swallow the anchor" (give up life at sea) or follow the siren call of piracy.

Rediker documented that between 1716 and 1726, the population of pirates ballooned to five thousand. They plundered aggressively and successfully. When Britain assigned warships to the Red Sea, pirates sailed to the Caribbean. The Bahamas replaced Madagascar as a pirate base.

Newport shipping was fair game.

From Pirate Patrons to Pirate Victims

Hawes gave a thorough account of Newporters victimized by pirates. Algerian pirates captured William Harris in 1638 and sold him into

One More Step Mr. Hands. N.C. Wyeth illustration. *From* Treasure Island, *by Robert Louis Stevenson.*

slavery. Harris was ransomed but died in London before he could return home. Piracy did not darken Newport's shores again until 1680 when Samuel Cranston, the future governor, was captured. A year later, the colony indicted, acquitted and banished four pirates. In 1682, Newport jailed several pirates. Some of them escaped after threatening to kill

Governor Sanford. But one pirate who was still in jail warned Sanford, and the governor survived the plot.

In the early eighteenth century, Caribbean pirates claimed numerous Newport victims. They included Governor Cranston's brother, Captain John Cranston; Boulston and Peter Coggeshall; and Captain Beer—the mariner released by Paulsgrave Williams. Benjamin Norton's controversial capture by Bartholomew Roberts also occurred during the postwar years.

Notorious Caribbean pirates Bartholomew Roberts, George Lowther, Ned (Edward) Low and Francis Spriggs preyed on English and colonial shipping. Since they attacked Newport's mariners, the colony wanted them to hang.

The Noose Tightened

After Queen Anne's War, England extended its naval patrols to Jamaica, the Bahamas and the Carolinas. London posted Royal Navy captains in almost all major port cities. When pirates ceased to be business partners, colonial governments turned their backs on them. With few friendly ports available, pirates became isolated and hunted.[29]

Prior to the 1700 Act of King William, captured pirates and their treasure had to be shipped to London. Captain Kidd's lengthy and expensive trial convinced Parliament that it would be in England's interest to allow colonial governments to try pirates.

In his book *Quelch's Gold*, Beal pointed out that Boston's 1704 trial of John Quelch and his crew was the first court of admiralty trial in New England. Britain's admiralty appointed local judges, sent a handful of officials to the colony, tried and executed the pirates in Boston. Colonial governors presided over vice-admiralty trials. Royal administrators and naval captains assisted.

Justice was swift. Governors, local administrators, naval captains and merchants had other affairs to attend to. Cordingly explained in *Under the Black Flag* that odds in piracy trials favored the authorities. Poorly educated seamen had to defend themselves. They usually claimed to be forced men and/or drunk when they signed the pirate ship's articles.

Pirate crews drew up and agreed to ship's articles. Men who could sign their name did so; others printed their initials or made their mark, and a literate crew member wrote the signee's name next to it. Prisoners who volunteered to join the pirates added their names to the articles. Forced recruits signed the articles at the point of a sword.

Accused pirates found themselves high and dry with the devil to pay. It is documented in *Between the Devil and the Deep Blue Sea* that England and its colonies executed between four and six hundred Anglo-American pirates from 1716 to 1726. Newport cooperated with the Royal Navy and vice-admiralty courts to capture, try and execute pirates. Once pirates turned against Newport, Newport turned against them.

12

Stretching Hemp for Pirates

Newport had its share of ropewalks—factories that produced hemp rope for the maritime trade. By the 1720s, Newport's hemp rope found its way to the gallows. Newporters occasionally "stretched hemp" for pirates and watched the condemned dance the "hempen jig."

The Gravelly Point Pirates

In 1723, Newport's Towne House, where the Colony House stands today, was the scene of Newport's first official admiralty court trial. It resulted in the largest mass execution in the colonies. On either July 17 or 19, reports vary, twenty-six pirates danced the hempen jig on Gravelly Point.

Twenty-five-year-old Charles Harris and his commander, the notorious Ned Low, sailed into Rhode Island waters. Mariners and the Royal Navy knew both sea-robbers. Captain Peter Solgard, commander of the *Greyhound*, a man-of-war stationed in New York, learned of the pirates' presence and set off in pursuit. His twenty-gun warship with 120 men sighted both their vessels off Block Island.

On June 14, Solgard lured the pirates into a chase. The *Boston Newsletter* reported the battle:

> Captain Solgard…steered…after them…the sloops giving us Chase…
> fired each a Gun, and hoisted a Black Flag…on the near approach of

The Rope Walk by Walter Francis Brown. *Courtesy of the Providence Art Club.*

the Man of War, they haul'd it down...and put up a Bloody Flag...
We hoisted up our Main-sail and made easy Sail to Windward, received
their Fire several times; but when abreast we gave them ours with round
& grape Shot, upon which the head Sloop edg'd away, as did the other
soon after...The Fire continued on both sides for about an hour; but when
they sail'd from us, with the help of their Oars, we left off Firing, and
turn'd to Rowing...we again kept close to Windward, and ply'd them
warmly with small and grape shot; during the Action we fell between
them, and having shot down one of their Main Sails we kept close to
him, and at 4 o Clock he called for Quarters...having got the Prisoners
on board, we continued to Chase the other Sloop...We lost sight of him
near Block Island. One Desperado was for blowing up this Sloop rather
than surrendering, and...with his Pistol shot out his own Brains.

The Two Pirate Sloops Commanded by the said Low and Harris
intended to have boarded the Man of War...but were discouraged, and
endeavoured all they could to escape.

Captain Low did escape. Solgard captured Captain Harris's *Ranger*
between Block Island and Long Island. The *Greyhound* took thirty-seven
white and six black prisoners. One prisoner, Thomas Mumford, was

a Martha's Vineyard Native American. The racial mix was typical of pirate ships.

New Englanders rejoiced at the news. Low and Harris had attacked local shipping for years. There would be ample evidence against Harris and his crew. A guilty verdict was assured.

Low was reputedly depraved, sadistic and cruel, but he proved to be cowardly and disloyal as well. He could have fought alongside Harris, but he chose to run. After escaping capture by the man of war, Low beheaded the captain of a fishing boat taken off Block Island. He cut out the heart of the captain of a Plymouth whaling sloop, roasted it and forced the captain's mate to eat it. He forced another captain to eat his own roasted ears before dying of his wounds. Justice caught up with Low. His crew, horrified by Low's brutal treatment of prisoners, turned against him. The *Boston Newsletter* reported crew members threw him into a small boat and abandoned him to his fate. Low was captured and hanged by the French.

During Low's murderous rampage, Captain Harris and thirty-five surviving crew members sat in Newport's jail. Officials from Massachusetts and Rhode Island took three weeks to organize a court of admiralty. Security was high—no cell doors would be left open for this crew.

The Trial

Nine judges, including Governor Cranston and John Menzies, presided. Menzies was the Massachusetts Admiralty Court judge who had a run-in with Governor Cranston over the Benjamin Norton episode, but this trial was too important for personal animosity to interfere with justice.

Witnesses' tales of capture and abuse at the hands of the pirates made the rounds of Newport's taverns. One witness, Captain Welland, arrived minus his right ear—Low had hacked it off. The court of public opinion indicted the *Ranger*'s crew before its trial began.

A three-foot-long silver oar, symbol of the admiralty, was traditionally placed before the court during trial and carried to the gallows. John Menzies probably brought the oar used at Quelch's Boston trial.

Captain Solgard, his lieutenant and his surgeon attested to the capture of the pirates. They accused the prisoners of attacking the *Greyhound* and wounding seven of its men. An advocate general for the king presented

State House, Newport by William Guy Wall. Gift of Hamilton Fish Webster and Lina Post Webster. *Courtesy of the Redwood Library & Athenaeum, Newport, Rhode Island.*

evidence regarding the seizure of Welland's *Amsterdam Merchant*, taking of its cargo, cutting off Captain Welland's right ear and sinking his ship.

Captain Welland recounted the details of his ship's capture and supported the claim of one of the pirates, his former crew member, of being a forced man. Welland identified six prisoners as having been harnessed—that is, well armed. Benjamin Weekham of Newport and William Marsh, both mariners, testified separately about being taken by Harris and Low and identified a number of the prisoners. When asked if they had anything to say in their own defense, the prisoners claimed the pirates forced them to join the crew.

Rhode Island's general assembly empowered field officers of the regiment of militia to order a military watch to secure the pirates in jail and set an appropriate penalty for not watching and securing the prisoners. In spite of that order, some prisoners escaped jail after the trial. The *Boston Newsletter* reported:

> *Three of the Condemned Pirates in our* [Newport] *Prison…got off their Irons; and when the Goal-Keeper* [sic]*, with a lusty young Man his Servant, and his Daughter open'd the Door where the Prisoners were, in order to give them their Breakfast, the said three Prisoners knock'd down*

the Goal-keeper [sic] *with their Irons, got out of the Goal* [sic] *and ran a little way to the out Skirts of the Town, but were speedily pursued and soon apprehended.*

Members of the clergy preached and prayed with pirates in prison. Reverend Clapp, head of the local Congregational Church, prayed and sermonized with the *Ranger*'s crew. Hattendorf noted that Reverend James Honyman, Anglican minister of Trinity Church, also assisted in their preparations for death. Years earlier, Royal Navy chaplain Honyman ministered to Captain Kidd on the HMS *Active*.

After three days of trial, the court reprieved two men and found eight not guilty. Fifteen-year-old Thomas Child was acquitted partly because of his age. One of the guilty, William Blades, a Rhode Island man, was the colony's only native son to be executed for piracy in Newport. Twenty-six Caribbean pirates danced the hempen jig.

The Execution

Admiralty executions had to be on or near the water, and they erected their gallows "between the flux and reflux" of the tides. That unsettled location guaranteed that the souls of the condemned would not find eternal peace.

Gravelly Point lies beneath the end of Long Wharf. In 1723, it was a spit of land that bounded the Basin, a body of water at the north end of the harbor. Long Wharf did not exist. Today's Point section was built on land brought in to fill the Basin.

No firsthand account of the execution has survived, but Beal's account of the 1704 Boston executions and Zacks's account of Kidd's London execution make it possible to imagine the event.

The *Ranger*'s captain and crew had their hands tied behind their backs at the elbows, not the wrists, since a dying man could free his hands. An armed guard led the condemned from prison, near the Towne House, to Gravelly Point. A single drummer, beating a funereal cadence, marched at the head of the procession over marshy terrain around the Basin. Either an admiralty judge or a local sheriff, carrying the miniature silver oar, followed the drummer on horseback. There is no record of payment to an admiralty judge, but the colony paid Sheriff J. Brenton £138.2 for "executing the Pyrates." Captain Harris marched in front of his crew. Militiamen armed

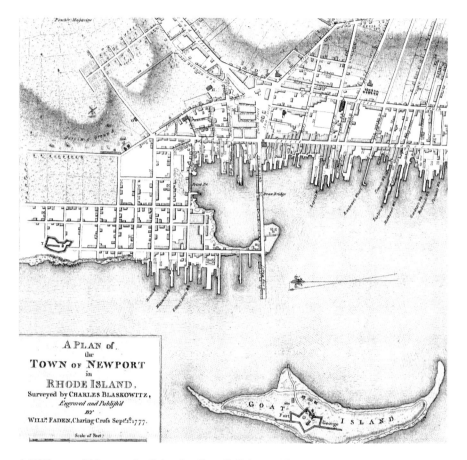

A 1777 map of Newport detail showing Gravelly Point and Goat Island (north is left). Charles Blaskowitz, surveyor. William Faden, London, printer. *Courtesy of Newport Historical Society.*

with muskets surrounded the condemned. Since both Reverend Clapp and Mr. Bass, a lay preacher, spoke at the gallows, they probably marched and prayed with the pirates.

A general holiday was proclaimed for public executions. Colonists from Maine to New York flocked to Newport. Business was brisk at Newport's taverns. Jeering onlookers hung out of windows and followed the procession on foot. Pickpockets worked the crowd. In London, revelers tossed dead dogs and cats covered with human excrement. Raucous laughter accompanied the landing of those vile missiles.

The best view of the gallows was from the Basin and the harbor. Overcrowded boats clustered near the shore. Men clung to the rigging and sat along the yards of ships anchored in Newport Harbor.

Workers sank two twelve-foot-high wooden poles into wet beach sand. They raised a pine log over the poles and lashed or nailed it in place. Ropes held a wide plank four or five feet above the base of the poles. Rope attachments allowed the platform to be released quickly. Nooses hung at shoulder level from the pine log.

There is no record of the size of the Gravelly Point gallows, but it would have been a large one. It is difficult to imagine it accommodating twenty-six men. Hanging the men shoulder to shoulder, allowing three feet per man, meant the gallows would have been an ungainly seventy-eight feet long. The largest gallows documented accommodated as many as nine prisoners, so three separate gallows might have been constructed. Or the pirates could have been executed in groups of nine on a single gallows. If that were the case, the platform and nooses would have been reassembled between hangings.

After a sermon and prayers, the condemned, with nooses around their necks, could address the crowd. Rowdy onlookers quieted down to hear the rogues' final words. A *Boston Newsletter* article reported:

> *Some of the Pirates that were, Executed…on the 19th…delivered what they had to say in Writing, which was read, or…recited; and most of them said something at the Place of Execution; advising all People, and especially Young Persons, to beware of the Sins which they had been guilty of, that had brought them into such unhappy Circumstances, and to so sad an end…Disobedience to Parents, profaning the Lord's Day, Swearing, Drinking, Gaming, Unchastity, and neglecting the Means of Grace by absenting themselves from the Public Worship of GOD.*

Executioners could use either a long or a short rope. A "long-drop" hanging broke the victim's neck, resulting in a quick death. It was merciful but not particularly entertaining. A "short-drop" hanging resulted in a slow death by strangulation. It could take as long as a half hour for life to be extinguished. Dangling legs jerked and danced the hempen jig until the soul departed. Since the prisoners' heads were not covered by dark hoods, onlookers watched their faces gradually turn purple. Just before death, the body's final release of urine stained the men's trousers. The crowd loved it.

The *Boston Newsletter* reported that the execution took place between twelve and two in the afternoon on Wednesday July 17. The pirates "were Executed under their own deep Blew Flagg which was hoisted up on their Gallows." The *New England Courant* gave a more complete account:

Mr. Bass went to Prayer with them…the Rev. Mr. Clap concluded with a short Exhortation to them. Their black Flag, with the Portrait of Death having an Hour Glass in one Hand, and a Dart In the other, at the end of which was the Form of a Heart with three Drops of Blood falling from it, was affix'd at one corner of the Gallows. This Flag they call'd Old Roger, and often used to say they would live and die under it.

The admiralty held them to that oath.

Three things that could happen at admiralty executions did not happen at Gravelly Point. None of the condemned received a last-minute reprieve, the pirates' corpses did not hang for the tide to wash over them three times and none of the pirates' corpses were gibbeted (hung in an iron cage) at the entrance to Newport Harbor.

Plaque at the end of Long Wharf marking the approximate location of Gravelly Point. *Photo by Helene Scola.*

Granting pardons to a criminal with a noose around his neck heightened the drama of the event. Authorities occasionally chose to do just that. Their reasons varied. The trial of Captain John Quelch and his crew resulted in seven guilty verdicts. After the prisoners mounted the gallows, an order from Governor Dudley was produced granting a reprieve to one of them. Beal explained that, since Quelch's trial was not popular, Dudley's dramatic demonstration of clemency was calculated to soothe public sentiment.

Admiralty custom required that pirates' corpses either be left hanging on the gallows or secured to posts until three successive high tides washed over them. A guard discouraged souvenir hunters and prevented families from stealing a body to give it a decent burial. There is no record that Newport paid guards to perform that duty or newspaper accounts to confirm that the custom was observed for the *Ranger*'s crew.

Decomposing bodies of pirates that were gibbeted at harbor entrances provided grisly evidence of how that port dealt with sea robbers. In 1726, Boston's court of admiralty sentenced Captain William Fly to death and stipulated that his body be gibbeted on an island in Boston Harbor. Captain William Kidd's sentence included the same stipulation. Kidd's corpse was displayed at Tilbury, where the Thames flows into the sea. There was no such order for Captain Charles Harris or any of his crew. In fact, there is no documented case of a pirate ever being gibbeted at the entrance to Newport Harbor.

Boats carried the pirates' corpses to the northern end of Goat Island, weighed them down with bags of sand and buried them between the high and low water mark. Only God-fearing citizens deserved to be well and decently interred. By two o'clock in the afternoon, the show was over.

After the execution, the *Boston Newsletter* listed thirty-five vessels taken by Harris and Low while John Walters, one of the condemned pirates, was on board. Benjamin Norton's sloop was on that list. Unlike Norton's previous capture by Bartholomew Roberts, there was no ambiguity regarding his capture by Harris and Low. A grateful New York rewarded Captain Solgard for capturing the *Ranger*. The *Boston Gazette* reported: "New York…presented Capt. Solgard with the Freedom of that City, handsomely express'd and finely engross'd with a Gold Snuff Box with the City Arms on one Side, and the Greyhound engaged with two Sloops on the other well Engraved with this Motto, viz. Quaesitos Humani Generii Hostes debellare Superbum. [He makes war proudly against enemies of the human race.]"

Boston's Reverend Cotton Mather was not in Newport for the trial or execution of the Gravelly Point pirates, but he collected information and

View of the north end of Goat Island, where the pirates were buried. The Newport Bridge is in the background. *Photo by Helene Scola.*

sold *An Account of the PIRATES with Divers of Their Speeches & Letters, Who Were Executed at NewPort off Rhode Island, July 19th 1723.* Clergymen sold censored accounts of pirate piety and repentance as lessons to anyone who might be "moved and seduced by the instigations of the Devil." The *Account* stated:

> *While they were in Prison, most of them seemed willing to be Advised, about the state of their Souls...Diverse of them lamentat [sic] their Disobedience to their Parents, & their Prophanation of the Name, Day and Word of God & their ungodly company Keeping; & warned Young People To Keep clear from those Crimes. And they did not Accept the Offers of Christ...and got...into the wild World, and then they Quickly got onto the High Road to Wickedness and Misery...They Ran away...from their Parents. They gave up themselves, To Drunkenness... Dishonesty, Evil speaking and Covetousness. And the most seemed to have no Thought of Returning from their wicked Course.*[30]

According to the *Account*, many of the pirates thanked God for bringing them to prison and giving them hope of forgiveness. They kept up something of daily religion and seemed "serious and reverent, while reading and hearing their prayers, and the Holy Scripture." An eyewitness observed there never was "a more Doleful Sight, in all this Land, than while they were standing on the Stage, waiting for the stopping of their Breath, and the Flying of their Souls into the Eternal World; And Oh! How Awful the Noise of their Dying Moans."[31]

A poem by John Fitz-Gerald, one of the condemned men, published posthumously, read in part:

To Mortal Men that daily live in Wickedness and Sin:
This dying Counsel I do give, hoping you will begin
To serve the Lord in Time of Youth his Precepts for to keep;
To serve him so in spirit and Truth, that you may mercy reap.

In Youthful blooming Years was I, when I that Practice took;
Of perpetrating Piracy, for filthy gain did look.
To Wickedness we all were bent, our Lusts for to fulfil;
To rob at sea was our Intent, and perpetrate all Ill.

I pray the Lord preserve you all and keep you from this End;
O let Fitz-Gerald's great downfall unto your welfare tend.
I to the Lord my Soul bequeath, accept thereof I pray,
My Body to the Earth bequeath, dear Friend, adieu for ay.[32]

Mutiny with Piratical Intent

Newport, Sept. 22. 1738. We are informed that the Sloop Dolphin…arrived at Block Island…and that her said Commander was kill'd by…Peter Legrand…and was thrown overboard by him and two other of the French Company…The said Legrand also murder'd an Englishman…and threw him overboard…After they came to Block-Island the said Legrand went into the Cabin and loaded two Pistols…and commanded one Thomas and John Merchant two Passengers on Board to throw over board a Boy….Nephew of said Capt…and if they refused they would shoot them immediately…[They] *threw the said Boy overboard, who was drowned…*[They] *are all secured in our Goal* [sic] *till they come to Tryal for such a barbarous Murder.*

The *Boston Newsletter* article quoted above sets the stage for Newport's next piracy trial. John Merchant informed the authorities of the French crew's murders and mutiny. Another passenger, Edward Sands of Block Island, would have been one of Mary and Edward Sands's (friends of Captain Kidd) relations, possibly a descendant.

The court claimed that Peter Legrand, Peter Iesseau and Francis Bandoine did

> *piratically and feloniously make a revolt in the said vessel against one Adam Dechezean…with a certain axe which he held in both his hands, piratically, feloniously, voluntarily, and of his malice aforethought, did assault and sundry times strike and wound upon his head, of which said striking and wounding he, the said Adam Dechezeau…did instantly die…and that the said Peter Iesseau and Francis Baudoine piratically, feloniously, voluntarily and of their malice aforethought…were present, aiding, assisting, abetting, encouraging and maintaining the said Peter Legrand in piratically and feloniously committing and perpetrating the aforesaid piracy, felony and murder.*[33]

Witnesses John Merchant and John Couprey presented evidence for the king. All three prisoners confessed. The sentence against them was pronounced in the following standard, bone-chilling words: "You, Peter Legrand, Peter Iesseau and Francis Baudoine shall go hence to the place from whence you came, and from thence you shall be carried to the place of execution, and then you and each of you shall be hanged up by the neck, until you and each of you are dead; and the Lord have mercy on your souls."[34]

The death sentence was carried out on Bull's Point, another name for Gravelly Point, within the flux and reflux of the sea.

The Not-So-Great Escape

A *Boston Newsletter* article referred to the July 23, 1760 appointment of commissioners "for the Examination of the Pirates confined in the Goal [*sic*] at Newport, Rhode Island, for the Sea robbery perpetrated on Capt. Honey, of the Schooner Frances." The article continued: "These Pirates sometime since their Commitment attempted to make their Escape, and effected it so far as to get out of the Goal [*sic*], and stealing a Boat, they

Newport Harbor, 1795, drawn by Samuel King, engraved by L. Allen. *Courtesy of Newport Historical Society.*

rowed in order to get on the Main, but being foggy they put ashore on the Fort [Goat] Island, and set their Boat adrift before they discovered their Mistake."

Easton's beach was the site of Parks's and Hawkins's execution.[35]

13
Ship's Articles

Evidence against pirates included whether or not the accused signed the ship's articles. Articles defined division of plunder, rules that governed the ship and punishment for offences. Pringle explained that privateers provided the model for pirates who drew up and voted on articles before each voyage and then swore to them on a Bible.

The Ranger's Articles

In August 1723, the *Boston Newsletter* reported Ned Low's articles. Since Low was the commander of the two ships, Harris and his crew would have signed Low's articles. The articles are as follows:

> *The Captain is to have two full Shares: the Master is to have one Share and one Half; The Doctor, Mate, Gunner and Boatswain, one Share and one Quarter.*
>
> *He that shall be found guilty of taking up any Unlawfull Weapon on Board the Privateer or any other prize by us taken, so as to Strike or Abuse one another in any regard, shall suffer what Punishment the Captain and Majority of the Company shall see fit.*
>
> *He that shall be found Guilty of Cowardice in the time of Ingagements [sic], shall suffer what Punishment the Captain and Majority of the Company shall think fit.*

If any Gold, Jewels, Silver, &c. be found on Board of any Prize or Prizes to the value of a Piece of Eight, & the finder do not deliver it to the Quarter Master in the space of 24 hours he shall suffer what Punishment the Captain and Majority of the Company shall think fit.

He that is found Guilty of Gaming, or Defrauding one another to the Value of a Ryal of Plate, shall suffer what Punishment the Captain and Majority of the Company shall think fit.

He that shall have the Misfortune to loose [sic] a Limb in time of Engagement, shall have the Sum of Six hundred pieces of Eight, and remain aboard as long as he shall think fit.

Good Quarters to be given when Craved.

He that sees a Sail first, shall have the best Pistol or Small Arm aboard of her.

He that shall be guilty of Drunkenness in time of Engagement shall suffer what Punishment the Captain and Majority of the Company shall think fit.

No Snaping [sic] of Guns in the Hould.

The articles ensured that every man pulled his weight, kept peace on board and provided for seriously injured mates, as well as ensured that no one blew up the ship. If possible, pirates threw articles overboard when it became clear that capture was imminent.

The High Road to Wickedness and Misery

Many deserters from the Royal Navy and merchant vessels voluntarily signed pirate ships' articles. Desertion was common for a number of reasons: abusive captains, low wages, poor rations and high mortality rate from disease. England's press gangs also played a role. Reluctant recruits had little or no sense of loyalty. In *Between the Devil and the Deep Blue Sea*, Rediker explained how press gangs operated.

Crimps and spirits pressed men into service. Crimps "recruited" men during England's wars. They raided pubs and handcuffed, dragged off and jailed drunken sailors before selling them to captains. Spirits regularly preyed on men not wise in the ways of the world, strangers to the big city and/or the unemployed. Spirits promised large wages and, occasionally, advanced money to potential "recruits." They might have paid off the debts of sailors before seizing them. Spirits either apprenticed their victims as sailors or sold them as indentured servants to America. Both crimps and spirits received the sailors' advance pay.

Navy captains also pressed men into service. As previously noted, a Royal Navy captain pressed Captain Kidd's best recruits before Kidd left the Thames. Naval vessels occasionally pressed Newport mariners into service as they entered their home port. That practice met with stiff resistance and added to the tensions that erupted in hostility against British enforcement ships during the second half of the eighteenth century.

While deserters found their way to pirate ships, prisoners arrived by accident. Pirates always offered prisoners the opportunity to sign on the account. Going on the account simply meant that no wages would be paid unless and until plunder was taken. The term was used for privateers as well as pirates.

Prisoners often met with a hard sell to encourage them to join the pirate crew. After Captain Beer's ship was sunk, Sam Bellamy did his best to convince the Newporter to sign up:

> D—— my Bl——d. I am sorry they won't let you have your Sloop again, for I scorn to do any one a Mischief, when it is not for my Advantage: damn the Sloop, we must sink her, and she might be of Use to you. Tho', damn ye, you are a sneaking Puppy, and so are all those who will submit to be governed by Laws which rich Men have made for their own Security, for the cowardly Whelps have not the Courage otherwise to defend what they get by their Knavery; but damn ye altogether; Damn them for a Pack of crafty Rascals, and you, who serve them, for a Parcel of hen-hearted Numskuls. They vilify us, the Scoundrels do, when there is only this Difference, they rob the Poor under the Cover of law, forsooth, and we plunder the Rich under the Protection of our own Courage: had you not better make One of us, than sneak after the A——s of these Villains for Employment?[36]

Captain Beer could not be convinced to "break thro' the Laws of God and Man." Bellamy continued his harangue:

> You are a devilish Conscience Rascal, d——n ye. I am a free Prince, and I have as much Authority to make War on the whole World as he who has a hundred Sail of Ships at Sea, and an Army of 100,000 Men in the Field; and this my Conscience tells me; but there is no arguing with such sniveling Puppies, who allow Superiors to kick them

about Deck at Pleasure; and pin their Faith upon a Pimp of a Parson: a Squab, who neither practices nor believes what he puts upon the chuckle-headed Fools he preaches to.[37]

Bellamy's colorful recruitment speech revealed pirates' views of Royal Naval officers, men of wealth and privilege and men of the cloth. He presented an unpleasant picture.

Pringle revealed that sailors who wanted to volunteer but were concerned about being caught sometimes secretly approached the quartermaster and asked him to "make a show" of forcing them. The quartermaster obliged with savage oaths and the slashing of cutlass. Fellow prisoners, not aware of the deception, could be witnesses in their mates' favor, should the recruits be captured. Another ruse involved the quartermaster giving forced crew members a certificate explaining they had been forced.

14

The Jolly Roger

Old Roger flew at the top of the gallows on Gravelly Point. It had a skeleton holding an hourglass in one hand and a dart in the other on a dark blue or black background. At the end of the dart was the form of a heart with three drops of blood falling from it.

Since pirates repaired their own sails, they could wield a sewing needle as well as a cutlass. They designed and made their own flags. Pirates preferred to throw their flag overboard if capture was imminent rather than see it flown above their gallows.

With the exception of cutlasses, scimitars, pistols and bleeding hearts, symbols from gravestone art—the skull, crossbones, skeleton and hourglass—dominated pirate flags. They communicated mortality and the limited amount of time available on earth. In Rediker's book *Villains of All Nations*, he explained that full skeletons represented King Death or the Grim Reaper. The names Jolly Roger, Old Roger and Roger referred to the devil. "Roger" in popular/vulgar usage was "a man's yard," or penis, and "to roger" meant to copulate. Jolly Roger and Old Roger, in strictly nautical usage, mean pirate flags of any design.

Flying Signals

Cordingly traced the evolution of pirate flags from naval and privateering signal flags. Pirates and privateers carried flags of different nations for use as a *ruse de guerre*, a deceptive practice designed to disguise their identity and lure prey by flying the flag of their country.

Pirates raised a red flag, the "bloody flag," to signal that any attempt to fight would result in death. The French called red flags *joli rouge*, or "pretty red." It is easy to imagine an English ear translating that to Jolly Roger.

A French flag book of 1721 defined the red flag to mean "no quarter would be given," a nautical phrase indicating that surrender was not possible. A ship called for quarter by waving a white flag.

A black flag warned of quarantine in the Royal Navy; however, privateers flew the black flag to signal that no quarter would be given. It evolved into the pirates' favorite flag, indicating theirs was an outlaw ship, not bound by the usual rules of engagement.

Captain John Quelch's 1704 trial provided one of the earliest accounts of a pirate flying Old Roger. His Old Roger resembled that of the *Ranger*'s crew. It had a skeleton in the middle with an hourglass in one hand and a dart piercing a heart with three drops of blood dripping from it in the other.

Skull and Crossbones

The skull and crossbones, a symbol of death, appear on many early tombstones, including that of Thomas Mallett in Trinity Church's graveyard. Captains sometimes drew them in ship's logs to record the death of a crew member.

Pringle noted that the black flag with white skull and crossbones alongside an hourglass was first recorded when a French pirate engaged a British

Thomas Mallett's gravestone in Trinity Church's cemetery. *Photo by Helene Scola.*

warship in 1700. Pirates adopted the symbol between 1700 and 1720. Later additions to the imagery include bleeding hearts, spears, cutlasses and pistols. Captain Thomas Tew's flag was black with a white arm wielding a scimitar. Sam Bellamy flew a black flag with a skull and crossbones when he chased Captain Prince on the *Whydah*. Pirates occasionally flew the Jolly Roger off the stern and a bloody flag or pennant from the mast.

Black flags with white or red symbols dominated the designs but exceptions existed. One French pirate's flag depicted a black death's head on a white ground.

Pirates used their flags to strike fear into the hearts of their opponents. A battle with those who fought under the Banner of King Death would be to the death.

15

Church and State

M en who sailed under the black flag captained their own souls. Their home, the oceans, separated them from the authority of both church and state. Sam Bellamy's recruitment speech fell on receptive ears more often than not. But royal officials and clergymen developed a recruitment strategy of their own.

The Pen and the Sword

Pirate wealth, swagger and heroic status dominated public opinion of pirates from the late seventeenth through the early eighteenth centuries. Parliament passed antipiracy laws and men of war attacked pirate ships, but victory would not have been possible without turning the tide of public opinion against the outlaws. Even as pirates drove the final nail into their coffins by attacking local shipping, officials left nothing to chance. Colonial American publications became a weapon in the war against piracy.

Ship captains made official reports of pirate attacks and of crew members forced to join pirates. Those reports provided evidence in favor of men who might later be captured and accused of volunteering. Newspapers published the information to make the public aware of family, friends and neighbors detained by pirates. Sea robbers stole more

Trinity Church, Newport by Helena Sturtevant. Gift of Hamilton Fish Webster and Lina Post Webster. *Courtesy of the Redwood Library & Athenaeum, Newport, Rhode Island.*

than cargo. They also stole the freedom of honest sailors. A *Boston Gazette* article of 1720 documented one such account:

> *These are to Certify, Edward Cain of Newport made Oath, That…he…was taken by a Pirate Ship & Sloop Commanded by One Roberts who forceably* [sic] *detained…George Bradly, Archibald Greenfield, & John Clinton all of Newport…Sworn before me this 10th Day of November 1720 at Newport Rhode Island.*

> *SAMUEL CRANSTON, Governor.*

During the Gravelly Point pirates' trial, prisoners John Libbey and Joseph Sweetser produced separate newspaper articles to back up their claim of being forced men. Libbey was found guilty, but Sweetser was acquitted.

Newspapers also helped locate and arrest pirates. In 1704, the *Boston Newsletter* published a proclamation from Governor Cranston to seize and apprehend pirates from John Quelch's crew. Cranston responded to a proclamation published days earlier by Lieutenant Governor Povey of Massachusetts. Povey reported that pirates fled from Boston to Newport, where five of them bought a boat and escaped. Thanks to Povey's initiative and Cranston's response, the sixth pirate was apprehended.

A generally illiterate public enjoyed having play-by-play reports of pirate captures read to them. The *Boston Newsletter*'s account of the *Ranger*'s capture was typical. Newspapers also published lists of accused pirates' names, ages and hometowns. After the trial, they printed the date of execution and the names of the condemned men, as well as those found not guilty. Interest was high, and printers made every attempt to profit from it.

Accounts of pirate cruelty provided valuable propaganda. Paulsgrave Williams was the subject of a June 1717 *Boston Newsletter* story: "Near one half of Paul William's the Pirate's Men were forced Men, who rose upon the Pirates, but did not succeed, five or six being dangerously wounded, and 'tis thought dyed [*sic*] within a few Days of their Wounds…It's said the Pirates condemned 3 of the forced Men to be hang'd."

Ned Low's behavior dispelled thoughts of pirates as heroes. Newspapers reported the gory details:

> Boston Newsletter, *July 1, 1723.*
> *The Pirates…abused the Men, Slit one of their Noses, Cut another over his cheek with a Cutlass, and broke the Nose of the third with the back of the same…'tis supposed to be Low.*

> Boston Newsletter, *June 21, 1723.*
> *We are informed from Nantucket The Pirate Low in a few Days after he parted with his Majesty's Ship the Greyhound, took a Nantucket Sloop…The Master of the Sloop that was taken was very barbarously Murdered by the Pirates…they cruelly whipt [sic] him about the Deck then they cut off his Ears; and after they had wearied themselves with making a game and sport of the poor Man; they told him, that because he was a good Master, he should have an easy Death and they shot him thro' the Head.*
> *…The Pirates had taken two Plymouth Vessels, and had Killed the Masters very Barbarously…by keeping the one alive and taking out his heart and roasting it and then made his Mate eat it, the other by slashing and mauling him, and then cutting of his Ears, they roasted them and made him eat them, who afterwards dyed [sic] of his Wounds.*

Benjamin Norton's merchant brigantine turned pirate ship played a role in a 1723 mutiny against pirates. The following *American Weekly Mercury* article would have encouraged prisoners to rise up against their captors:

> *We have advice that…the Pyrate Captain and some of the Pyrates some forced Men and some free Negros were left on board the Pyrate Brigantine (which formerly belonged to one Norton of Rhode Island) the forced Men rose upon the Pyrates kill'd the Captain and some others and carried the Brigantine into Coracoa, with the Captains Head in a Tarr Bucket.*

Pirates who survived capture with their heads attached met with both civil and divine justice.

City of God, City of Man

Trinity Church's rector, William Smith, explained the role of civil magistrates: "The law is made for the lawless and disobedient. By the law is the knowledge of sin; and sin is the transgression of the law. The civil magistrate beareth not the sword in vain; for he is the minister of God, a revenger to execute wrath upon him that doeth evil."[38]

God's earthly ministers—magistrates and clerics—served the city of man in different capacities, but they served the same master.

Admiralty court trials documented the dispensation of justice—both civil and divine. London's royal court of admiralty ordered full accounts of judicial proceedings against pirates. Printers discovered that the public also wanted to read trial reports. Boston's 1704 trial documented in *The Arraignment, Trial, and Condemnation of Captain John Quelch and Others of His Company for Sundry Piracies, Robberies, and Murder* was one example. *The Trials of Eight Persons Indited* [sic] *for Piracy* recorded the proceedings against Sam Bellamy's surviving crew. A Boston printer published *The Trial of Thirty-six Persons Indicted for Piracy*, an account of the Gravelly Point pirates' trial.

Tryals of Thirty Six Persons for Piracy Newport, R.I. 1723. Ink on paper. RIHi X17 1697. Samuel Kneeland printer, Boston. *Courtesy the Rhode Island Historical Society.*

Notches on Their Bibles

The clergy's calling was to save souls, and members took their task seriously. Condemned pirates provided ministers with captive audiences for hellfire-and-brimstone sermons, prayer vigils and relentless pleas for repentance. Local clergy and lay preachers visited the prisoners before, during and after their trials. They continued their ministrations along the march to the gallows, at the site of execution and as the pirates' souls launched into eternity.

London set the example for clerics to minister to capital criminals. Newgate jail, where Captain Kidd was held, employed a full-time chaplain. According to Zacks, it was a highly sought-after position. Accounts of pirates' dying speeches sold well. Chaplain Paul Lorraine made a tidy profit from his *Account of the Behavior, Confession and Death of Captain William Kidd, and Other Pirates*. Lorraine had a monopoly on Kidd while the accused pirate was a prisoner, but not while he was at the foot of the gallows. A collection of ministers vied for the privilege of saving Kidd's soul at Execution Dock. Lorraine had the advantage of being able to claim that success in print.

Boston's Reverend Cotton Mather was the best-known colonial preacher to subject incarcerated pirates to relentless sermonizing, prayer sessions and pleas for repentance. His published accounts of pirates' warnings sounded like sermons from the time. One member of the *Ranger*'s crew, quoted in Mather's *Account of the Pirates*, wrote:

> *O that it may please the great and glorious God of Heaven and Earth! to give every one of you Grace to avoid the Snares I have Fallen into. Youths. Early fear God and honour and obey your Parents…Let not the vain notion of Rambling contrary to their Will take any Root in your Heart and Mind…Whatever you do, neglect not the public and private Worship of God…Always choose good company…live soberly…Beware the abominable Sin of Uncleanness…Suffer not the least Spark of that infernal Fire of Lust…Take Care against spending your Time idly on the Sabbath Day…frequent your proper Places of divine Worship, respect your Parents and Teachers, and remember whose Servants they be, and pay the just Deference due to the Rulers set over you by God…Stay in your Place and Station contently.*[39]

In other words, obey superiors, know one's place and don't make trouble. Sam Bellamy's comments about "cowardly whelps," "hen-hearted

Numbskuls," "sniveling Puppies" and "Pimp of a Parson" make it easy to imagine his response to that pirate's warning.

The combined forces of church and state relied on those warnings to save mariners from temptation. Cotton Mather regularly admonished his flock to mind the story, lest you make the story. Public executions took sermons from the pulpit to the gallows. Pirates exemplified how great God's grace was to save even the most vile, penitent sinners among us.

In 1717, Cotton Mather wrote in his diary: "What I now think of, is; how to render the Condition of the poor Pyrates, who are coming on their Trial, serviceable unto the Interests of Piety in the world."[40] In another diary entry Mather asked: "May not I do well to give the Bookseller, something that may render the Condition of the Pirates, lately executed, profitable?"[41]

Mather did render the condition of pirates profitable. His published execution sermons—with additional comments on the pirates' pleas for forgiveness, fear and trembling on the gallows and dying cries—expanded both his audience and his purse. Mather wrote a sermon inspired by the Gravelly Point pirates' ordeal. He delivered *An Essay upon Remarkables in the Way of Wicked Men: A Sermon on the Tragical End, unto Which the Way of Twenty-Six Pirates Brought Them; At New Port on Rhode Island, July, 19, 1723* to his Boston congregation and then published it for the greater good.

Public executions and the sermons they inspired combined to create a secular and religious ritual intended to cleanse the community of evil and avoid God's wrath. The ritual's meaning derived from the belief that individual transgression equaled collective transgression. Society needed to be purged of its sinfulness. Executing criminals helped achieve that goal. Executing them publicly gave good Christians the opportunity to witness the vile nature of pirates and receive a living lesson on the evils of sin, promise of repentance and hope of forgiveness.

Pirates had a starring role in the morality play that was their execution. Their road to repentance and salvation began in jail and culminated on the gallows. Once the noose was placed around their necks, many pirates delivered an emotional acknowledgement of guilt, a heartfelt repentance and a plea for God's mercy. If pirates played their part well, they provided examples to the community of reformed sinners and could hope for salvation.

Some pirates cooperated. Some did not.

Dying Breath

Quelch's crew members followed Mather's path to salvation. When John Miller's neck was in a noose, he cried out, "Lord, What shall I do to be Saved!" John Lambert's last words were, "Lord, forgive my Soul! Oh, receive me into Eternity! Blessed Name of Christ receive my Soul." Captain Quelch spoke his mind: "What I have to say is this, I desire to be informed for what I am here, I am Condemned only upon Circumstances. I forgive all the World: So the Lord be Merciful to my Soul." When one of his crew warned against keeping bad company, Quelch shouted to the spectators that "they should also take care how they brought Money into New-England, to be Hanged for it!"[42]

Cotton Mather's greatest challenge was William Fly. The pirate murdered his abusive captain and led his crew in mutiny. Fly did not bow before court or clergy and was arrogant during his trial and disdainful of the proceedings.

Fly's crew cursed Dr. Mather when they sailed, but after arrest, they requested Mather's counsel and chose him to deliver their execution sermon. All but their captain followed Mather's road to repentance.

Mather's Christianity taught submission to authority. Fly's life taught him self-reliance and loyalty to his pirate brethren. Fly did not confess and beg forgiveness from the scaffold. In his article "Puritans and Pirates," Williams related that Fly's exit speech did not warn against following him in sin, but warned ship's captains not to abuse their men and risk murder and mutiny at their hands.

Fly would have enjoyed the "penitence" of a pirate crew executed in the Bahamas. When told to turn his mind "to another World, and sincerely to repent," an account detailed the pirates' responses: "[One said,] 'I do heartily repent; I repent I had not done more Mischief, and that we did not cut the Throats of them that took us, and I am extremely sorry that you an't hanged as well as we.' 'So do I,' says another: 'And I,' says a third."[43]

The executioner sent the pirates to their final reward before they could repent further.

Some pirates sought salvation at the gallows. Others reformed themselves without ever having had their neck in a noose. A number of Newport's sea robbers proved that piracy and piety were not mutually exclusive.

16

Trinity Church

Sixteen petitioners requested an Anglican minister for Newport's Trinity Church. They asked Lord Bellomont to intercede with His Majesty on their behalf. Bellomont, who investigated three of the petitioners' connections to piracy, was happy to oblige. He believed the presence of an Anglican minister in Newport would help reform the city's citizens. Five of the petitioners had dicey reputations.

Paine and Cutler

Retired pirates Captain Thomas Paine and George Cutler married into respectable Newport families and led exemplary post-pirating lives. Fellow Christians proudly signed their names alongside those of Cutler and Paine. None of the other petitioners sailed under the black flag, but they conducted business and socialized with those who did.

Thomas Mallett

Newport's innkeeper and sheriff Thomas Mallett entertained pirates at his Clarke Street Inn. Sion Arnold, Richard Cornish and James Gillam all enjoyed Mallett's hospitality.

Trinity Church Founders' Stone at church entrance. *Photo by Helene Scola.*

Thomas Mallett is buried in Trinity Church's graveyard. The tribute on his gravestone reads, "He was a father to ye fatherless" and reveals that Mallett's contemporaries thought highly of the innkeeper.

Robert Gardner

Robert Gardner is buried near Thomas Mallett. The inscription on his gravestone makes it clear that he was well respected by his fellow Christians: "Here lieth interred the body of Mr. Robert Gardner, Esq., who was one of the first promoters of the church in this place; he survived all his brethren and had the happiness to see this church completely finished. He was a naval officer and collector of this port for many years, also employed in the affairs of this colony, and discharged his trust to satisfaction."

Lord Bellomont held a different opinion of the deputy collector. He complained about Gardner to the board of trade regarding his possession of Gillam's gold and accused the deputy collector of having been a pirate. The earl also investigated Gardner's connection with the *Pelican*, a 1696 French prize. Hawes explained that Captain Colly, a Jamaican privateer, captured the *Pelican* off Newfoundland and brought it to Newport for condemnation. While in Newport, Colly and his quartermaster made Gardner their

Trinity Church Newport, RI by John Perry Newell. Gift of Hamilton Fish Webster and Lina Post Webster. *Courtesy of Redwood Library & Athenaeum, Newport, Rhode Island.*

attorney. Colly assumed command of the *Pelican* and received a privateering commission from Governor Clarke to capture French ships on his way back to Jamaica, but Jamaica was not on Colly's itinerary. He sailed the *Pelican* to Madagascar instead .

Everyone knew Colly intended to go to the Red Sea. Gardner's dealings with Colly reflected the wink-and-nod attitude toward pirates during the late seventeenth century, Thomas Tew's glory days when "it was no sin to kill" infidels. Gardner gave Mayes, captain of the *Pearl*, and Bankes, commander of the *Portsmouth Adventure*, clearances to sail on Tew's second Red Sea voyage. No one doubted their piratical intentions.

Robert Wrightington

Both Robert Gardner and Robert Wrightington conducted business with pirates. Wrightington had the additional distinction of his stepson's being accused of piracy.

Wrightington possibly crewed as a privateer with Captain Colly, but he remained in Newport when Colly sailed to the Red Sea. Captain Robert Withington, at whose home Robert Munday was arrested, was probably Robert Wrightington. Wrightington sold a brigantine to Peter Brock, former pirate and Newport sheriff who also worshipped at Trinity Church.

Wrightington married Margaret (Ward) Bradley, the older sister of pirate Sion Arnold's wife. Margaret had a son by a previous marriage, George Bradley Junior.[11] A 1720 *Boston Gazette* article, quoted earlier, reported that Bartholomew Roberts forcibly detained four men, including George Bradley. Bradley left a young wife and child in Newport.

George Bradley's name appeared on a petition sent to London claiming that Roberts forced them to serve as pirates. The petition, printed in the *New England Courant*, read in part:

> *That we your Majesty's most Loyal Subjects, have…been taken by Bartholomew Roberts…and have been forced by him and his wicked Accomplices to enter into, and serve in the said Company as Pirates, much contrary to our Wills and Inclination. And we your Loyal Subjects utterly abhorring and detesting that impious way of living did with unanimous Consent, and contrary to the Knowledge of said Roberts or his Accomplices…leave and run away…with…the hopes of obtaining your Majesty's most gracious Pardon.*

The petitioners signed their names around a circle, known as a round robin, to avoid possible identification of leadership.

While the men waited for news of their pardon, they amused themselves with a mock trial that was recorded in DeFoe. The pirates assumed the role of judge, attorneys and prisoners. George Bradley played the role of judge.

Bradley never returned to Newport and might have been executed. His wife is buried in Newport's Common Burying Ground, but no record of George Bradley's burial exists.

Bradley's uncle, Richard Ward, recorder for the colony, was paid six pounds for attending the execution of the Gravelly Point pirates.[15] Only a few degrees of separation existed between Newport's citizens.

17

Pirates and Revolutionaries

Newport's citizens' reputation as a lawless and piratical people endured into the late eighteenth century, but the citizens countered with accusations of their own.

John Valentine, advocate general for the Gravelly Point pirates' trial, defined piracy for the court:

> *The crime of piracy is a robbery (for piracy is the sea term for robbery) committed within the jurisdiction of the admiralty.*
>
> *And a pirate is described to be one who to enrich himself either by surprise or open force, sets upon merchants and others trading by sea to spoil them of their goods and treasure, often times by sinking their vessel.*[46]

In the years leading up to the American Revolution, both the colonists and England accused one another of piracy.

Beginning in 1764, London placed armed ships in American harbors to eliminate smuggling and collect taxes. Enforcement ships chased, boarded and confiscated colonial vessels and their cargoes. Writs of Assistance (general warrants to enforce revenue laws) allowed His Majesty's officers to enter any place, house or boat, to search for and seize illicit goods without probable cause. Abuse of authority was rampant. The Fourth Amendment to the U.S. Constitution prohibiting unreasonable search and seizure was inspired, in part, by British harassment of colonial shipping.[47]

Arrogant commanders and heavy-handed tactics angered Newporters. His Majesty's officers pressed Newport men into service and seized trading vessels and their goods. Violent clashes erupted between Newport's citizens and British enforcement ships.

His Majesty's Schooner St. John

In 1764, the British enforcement ship *St. John* seized a brig and brought it into Newport. That act in itself was offensive, but the attempt by the ship's crew to press sailors into service led to a dockside brawl and the firing of Fort George's guns on the *St. John*. A July 16, 1764 *Newport Mercury* article described what happened:

> *Some Men belonging to his Majesty's Schooner* St. John*…had been guilty…of some Irregularities in Town. A Boat with some Men armed, came in…to impress Men at Work on board a Vessel…A smart Skirmish was the Consequence…the Schooner's Men were considerably bruised…went off, leaving their commanding Officer behind, who was immediately taken into Custody.*

Newport in 1730. An 1884 lithograph by John Perry Newell showing Fort George on Goat Island and Gravelly Point beyond. *Courtesy of Newport Historical Society*.

The men refused to surrender to Newport's authorities. Fort George on Goat Island received orders to stop the schooner. When the *St. John* appeared to be sailing out of the harbor, it was hailed from the fort but ignored the order to stop. The gunner fired, and *St. John* took refuge behind a man-of-war. Captain Smith, commander of the warship, delivered the offending crew members to Newport's authorities. Their fate was not reported.

Opening fire on the *St. John* might have been the first colonial attack against one of His Majesty's ships, but it was not the last English vessel attacked in Newport Harbor.

His Majesty's Ship Maidstone

One year after the attack on *St. John*, a mob stole a boat from the dock: "Tuesday Evening last…his Majesty's Ship the *Maidstone*'s Boat was taken from one of the Wharves, by a Mob consisting chiefly of Sailors, Boys and Negroes, to the Number of above Five Hundred, haul'd up through Queen-Street to the Common…where they burnt her."

Those are the opening lines of an opinion piece published on June 10, 1765, in the *Newport Mercury*. The *Maidstone* was a British naval vessel that impressed seamen in Newport Harbor. Its monthlong presence resulted in ships avoiding the harbor. The opinion piece continued:

> [They] *have visited every Vessel entering the Harbour, our Wood Boats, and the very smallest Coasters…to impress Men, and have generally taken all* [men] *that did not belong to the Town of Newport, as Capt. Antrobus had given his Word to the Sheriff that he would take none of those; yet the Consequence of these arbitrary and illegal Measures, especially in Time of profound Peace, proves as fatal to the Inhabitants of the Town…our Wood Wharves almost clear of Wood, the Coasters from the neighbouring Governments shunning our Port, to escape the hottest Press ever known in this Town…the Coasters, who supply the Inhabitants with Necessaries of Life, driven from our Harbour…Our Fish Market, a considerable Support of the Town is greatly distressed, as few of the Fishermen dare venture out.*

Colony House and Parade by John Collins, from *The City and Scenery of Newport, Rhode Island*, NJ. 1857. *Courtesy of the Redwood Library & Athenaeum, Newport, Rhode Island.*

The *Maidstone*'s activity blockaded Newport Harbor. When it pressed the entire crew of a returning brig, Newporters resorted to an open act of piracy—they stole the *Maidstone*'s skiff from a dock, dragged it to the Common (Washington Square) and torched it in front of the Colony House.

Torching the king's vessels became one of Newport's favorite acts of resistance.

The Armed Sloop Liberty

Newporters torched the *Maidstone*'s skiff in 1765. Four years later, they set fire to their first ship.

During the summer of 1769, the *Liberty*, commanded by William Reid, harassed shipping from Long Island Sound to Narragansett Bay. Reid captured a brig and a sloop out of Connecticut and brought them into Newport. His crew's abuse of the brig's captain angered Newport's citizens. A contemporary writer described what happened:

A few Days ago an armed Sloop in the Service of the Revenue…commanded by…William Reid, arrived in this Port…brought in with her a Brigantine… commanded by —— Packwood, and a Sloop…On the same Cruize the vigilant Reid took one of the Providence Packet Boats & sent her to Boston or Halifax.

   Last Wednesday in the afternoon Capt. Packwood went on Board his Brig in Order to take a Shore his Wearing Apparel and finding his Things turned out of the Cabbin he manifested his Surprise at it to the officer…The officer damned him; told him he had a right to do what he pleased on Board that Vessel; that he (Packwood) should not carry anything out of her, and treated him with such abusive, scandalous, threatening language, that Capt. Packwood…drew his Sword…and told him that if he persisted in his insolent Behavior he would infallibly run him through…[Captain Packwood] *had no sooner left the Brigantine's Side…*[than the officer] *ordered* [the cutter] *to fire upon that damned Rascal…Packwood got safe to the Long Wharf.*[48]

People assembled on the wharf to hear Packwood's story. Their resentment was inflamed against Captain Reid's harassment of local shipping and seizing a Providence packet boat, as well as by the attempts by the customs officer to collect higher fees than he was entitled to. They decided that:

Satisfaction should be made to Capt., Packwood, & that a temporary Check at least should be given to the mercenary, piratical Conduct of Capt., Reid…that he would deliver up the Person who fired at Capt., Packwood…Part of the People hauled up the Liberty's *Boats carried them off and burned them, and Part of them went on Board* Liberty *Sloop. Cut her Cable, and let her go ashore, when they went to work deliberately and scuttled, dismasted, stripped and dismantled her.*[49]

Reid's "piratical conduct" consisted of seizing a local boat without cause and sending it to another port for condemnation. The people who ransacked the *Liberty* and destroyed its boats also committed acts of piracy.

During the mêlée, the sloop brought in by Reid quietly left the harbor. Captain Packwood's brig cleared customs the next day and sailed for New York.

Two *Newport Mercury* articles reported on the *Liberty's* ultimate fate. The first was printed on July 31, 1769: "Last Saturday the sloop *Liberty* was floated by a high tide, and drifted over to Goat Island, and is grounded at the north

Washington Square, circa 1818, artist unknown. *Courtesy of the Newport Historical Society.*

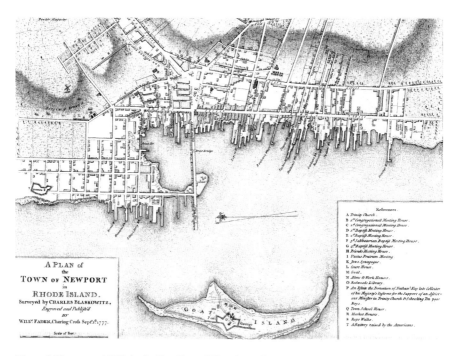

Map of Newport, 1777, including Long Wharf, the Basin, Gravelly Point and Goat Island. Charles Blaskowitz, surveyor. William Faden, London, printer. *Courtesy of Newport Historical Society.*

end, near the place where the pirates were buried. What this prognostigates we leave to the determination of astrologers."

Newporters no doubt agreed with the *Mercury*'s thinly veiled comparison of Reid's behavior to that of the Gravelly Point pirates. The second article appeared on August 7: "Last Monday evening, just after the storm of rain, hail and lightning the sloop *Liberty*, which we mentioned in our last as having drifted to Goat Island, was discovered to be on fire, and continued burning several days, until almost entirely consumed."

Governor Wanton issued a proclamation for the arrest of those responsible. It was published in the *Newport Mercury*:

> *Whereas William Reid Commander of the Sloop* Liberty, *employed in the Service of His Majesty's Customs, having made Seizure of a Sloop named the* Sally…*loaded with a Cargo of prohibited Goods, carried the same into the Harbor of Newport, Rhode Island, where a great Number of People riotously and tumultuously assembled together in the Evening of the 19ᵗʰ of July last, and having, by Force and Arms, attacked and secured the said Captain Reid and his Men, and taken Possession of both Vessels; they set Fire to, and sunk the* Liberty, *and carried off the Sloop* Sally.

Governor Wanton offered a reward to anyone who identified the guilty parties. No one was arrested.

Arnold asserted that the burning of the *Liberty* was the first overt act of violence against the British in America. The burning of the *Gaspee* would be the second.

The Gaspee Affair

Lieutenant Duddingston brought the schooner *Gaspee* to Narragansett Bay in 1772. Duddingston's relentless pursuit of everything afloat brought harassment of local shipping to a new level. He interfered with market boats and plundered people on shore without showing his commission, an act that violated Rhode Island's charter,

In March, Duddingston seized the sloop *Fortune* and discovered that its commander had not claimed his cargo in Newport. In defiance of Rhode Island's charter and an act of Parliament that required captured vessels to be tried locally, Duddingston sent his prize to Boston for condemnation.

Deputy Governor Darius Sessions addressed his concerns to Governor Joseph Wanton:

> *She* [the Gaspee] *suffers no vessel to pass…they are compelled to submit by armed force. Who he is and by what authority he assumes such a conduct, it is thought needs some inquiry.*
>
> *…It is suspected he has no legal authority to justify his conduct and his commission…I have consulted with the Chief Justice…who is of the opinion that no commander of any vessel has any right to use any authority in the Body of the Colony without previously applying to the Governor and showing his warrant.*[50]

Governor Wanton had a letter delivered to the "commanding officer of a schooner near Brenton's Point":

> *Sir:—A considerable number of the inhabitants of this Colony have complained to me of your having, in a most illegal and unwarrantable manner, interrupted their trade, by searching and detaining every little packet boat…produce me your commission and instructions, if any you have, which was your duty to have done when you first came within the jurisdiction of this Colony.*[51]

Duddingston sent Wanton's letter to Admiral Montagu, commander in chief of his Majesty's fleet. Montagu informed Governor Wanton that Duddingston was "on that station to protect your province from pirates and to give the trade all the assistance he can, and…to protect the revenue officer, and to prevent…the illicit trade that is carrying on at Rhode Island." Montague continued, saying, "I am also informed, the people of Newport talk of fitting out an armed vessel to rescue any vessel the King's schooner may take…Let them be cautious what they do; for as sure as they attempt it, and any of them are taken, I will hang them as pirates."[52]

Wanton responded, "[Duddingston] at no time…showed me any orders from the admiralty or from you, and positively denied that he derived any authority either from you or the commissioners; therefore, it was altogether out of my power to know, whether he came hither to protect us from pirates or was a pirate himself."[53]

Things went downhill from there: "On the 10th day of June, 1772, Capt. Thomas Lindsey left Newport…for Providence…and soon after the

Gaspee was under sail in pursuit… and continued the chase as far as Namcut Point…[Lindsey] hove about at the end of Namcut Point…and Duddingston, in close chase…ran on the point…and grounded."[54]

Colonel Ephraim Bowen, quoted above, recounted the events of one of Rhode Island's proudest acts of rebellion—the destruction of the hated *Gaspee*. It was aground and helpless in Narragansett Bay about seven miles out of Providence. Captain Lindsey arrived in Providence at sunset and immediately informed John Nicholas Brown, a respected merchant and namesake of Brown University, of the *Gaspee*'s

Governor Joseph Wanton, artist unknown. Gift of Angelica Gilbert Gardiner. *Courtesy of the Redwood Library & Athenaeum, Newport, Rhode Island.*

predicament. It would be past midnight before the high tide freed the *Gaspee*. The good citizens of Providence seized the opportunity:

> *Mr. Brown immediately resolved on her destruction, and he forthwith directed one of his trusty shipmasters to collect eight of the largest long-boats in the harbor, with five oars to each, to have the oars and row-locks muffled to prevent noise…a man passed along the Main street beating a drum, and informing the inhabitants of the fact, that the* Gaspee *was aground on Namcut Point, and would not float off until 3 o'clock the next morning, and inviting those persons who felt a disposition to go and destroy that troublesome vessel…About 9 o'clock I took my father's gun, and my powder-horn and bullets, and went to Mr. Sabin's, and found the south-east room full of people, where I loaded my gun, and all remained there till about 10 o'clock, some casting bullets in the kitchen, and others making arrangements for departure…a sea-captain acted as steersman…of whom I recollect Capt. Abraham Whipple…and Capt. Hopkins.*[55]

The *Gaspee*'s sentinel shouted to the approaching boats. Captain Whipple answered, "I am sheriff of the county of Kent, God damn you, I have got a warrant to apprehend you, God damn you, so surrender, God damn you."[56] Captain Duddingston appeared on deck. A shot was fired, and Duddingston fell. The Providence boats drew alongside the *Gaspee* and boarded it. One of the boarding party, John Mawney, a medical student, attended to Duddingston. The captain survived his wounds.

Colonel Bowen described the *Gaspee*'s ultimate fate: "Soon after, all the party were ordered to depart, leaving one boat for the leaders of the expedition, who soon set the vessel on fire, which consumed her to the waters edge."[57]

The day after the attack, Governor Wanton received a letter from Admiral Montagu:

> *Enclosed I transmit* [to] *your Excellency a deposition taken before me of the piratical proceedings of the people of Providence in Rhode Island government, by attacking his Majesty's schooner with an armed force, wounding her commander in a dangerous manner, and then setting her on fire…your Excellency will use such methods as you shall think proper for apprehending and bringing the offenders to justice.*[58]

William Dickenson, the deposed crew member of the *Gaspee* referred to by Montague, revealed that after Duddingston was wounded "the two ringleaders…came to him and said, 'Now you piratical rascal, we have got you. Damn you, we will hang you all by the laws of Great Britain…' The captain [of the ringleaders]…said, 'Stand aside and let me dispatch the piratical dog.'" Dickenson continued, saying, "The ringleaders…demanded his [Duddingston's] papers and orders for his proceeding in such piratical manner."[59]

Governor Wanton issued a proclamation offering a reward to any "Person or Persons who shall discover the Perpetrators of the said Villany." Wanton's action pleased Montagu. He wrote to the governor: "I am…much obliged for the part you have taken in endeavoring to find out and bring to justice, those rebellious, lawless, and piratical people who were concerned in wounding the King's Lieutenant and burning his schooner."[60]

According to James in his book *Colonial Rhode Island*, setting fire to one of his majesty's ships was a crime punishable by death. Colonists accused of the crime would be tried in England. The burning of the *Gaspee* was that law's test case.

London asserted that the robbery and plunder of the *Gaspee* was not only an act of piracy but also one of high treason. King George charged a commission to hold a secret board of inquiry that would gather evidence

Burning of the Gaspee, engraving. *From* Harper's New Monthly Magazine, *no. 399 (August 1883).*

and consider how to proceed. Governor Wanton was one of four men named to that commission. Governor Wanton informed his assembly of his appointment to the king's secret board of inquiry. In *Narragansett Bay*, Bacon explained that the Rhode Island assembly, meeting in Newport, leaked the information to the press.

An article appeared in the *Newport Mercury* in January 1773:

> The public are hereby informed that the Honorable the Commissioners appointed…under the great seal of Great Britain, for inquiring into the circumstances of attacking, plundering, and burning, His Majesty's schooner the Gaspee…are now convened, and continue to set every day, Sundays excepted, at the Colony House, in Newport: Wherefore all persons, who can give information to the said Commissioners, relative to the attacking, plundering and burning His Majesty's said schooner…are requested, forthwith, to give information thereof to said Commissioners.

Everyone knew the guilty parties, but no one was arrested.

The *Gaspee* affair, as it is still referred to in Rhode Island, began when Lieutenant Duddingston chased the *Hannah* from Newport to Providence. It concluded when royally appointed commissioners convened at Newport's Colony House. While Newporters did not participate in the burning of the *Gaspee*, they cheered the ship's destruction.

Rhode Islanders continue to cheer the burning of the *Gaspee* to this day. An annual monthlong celebration of *Gaspee* Days culminates in mid-June with fireworks, a parade and a symbolic burning of the *Gaspee*. Namquid Point was renamed Gaspee Point in honor of the event.

Captain Abraham Whipple, a leader in the attack, was one of John Brown's merchant captains. A 1774 confrontation between Abraham Whipple and Sir James Wallace, captain of an enforcement ship, resulted in Whipple capturing one of Wallace's small boats. An indignant Wallace wrote, "You, Abraham Whipple, on the 10th of June, 1772, burned His Majesty's vessel, the *Gaspee*, and I will hang you at the yard-arm."

Abraham Whipple replied, "To Sir James Wallace, Sir: Always catch a man before you hang him. Abraham Whipple."[61]

Whipple's admirable response summed up the colony's defiant attitude toward England. He became a privateer captain and hero of the Continental navy. In 1775, Captain Whipple was put in command of the *Washington* and the *Katy*, the first two ships of the colonial navy. The *Katy*, one of John Brown's merchant vessels, was renamed the *Providence*.

Continental Sloop Providence. *Photo by Helene Scola.*

Newport Harbor is the home port of Rhode Island's official flag ship, a replica of the Continental sloop *Providence*.

According to Hawes, Rhode Island issued 140 privateering commissions during the Revolutionary War. The privateers these commissions empowered took a heavy toll on English commerce. A June 1812 comment in the *London Statesman* made it clear that London respected colonial privateers: "America has nearly 100,000 as good seamen as any in the world…They possess nautical knowledge, with equal enterprise to ourselves…In a predatory war on commerce, Great Britain would have more to lose than to gain."[62]

Many of Rhode Island's Revolutionary War privateers descended from Newport's early mariners. Their ancestors might have been pirates and/or privateers who sailed in and out of piracy's dark waters. Abraham Whipple may have descended from Captain John Whipple, or his brother, Joseph Whipple, owner of Benjamin Norton's captured brigantine. Joseph Whipple became deputy governor of Rhode Island. A later Benjamin Norton, possibly the son of the captured Norton, captained a legitimate privateer in 1741. His great-grandson Professor Charles Elliott Norton taught at Harvard University.[63] It was difficult for Newport families to avoid sharing the occasional gene with a pirate.

England justifiably accused the men who attacked its enforcement ships of piracy. Heavy-handed royal officials, also guilty of piracy, drove the colonists to do what they did.

Newport's early colonial sea robbers pirated for profit, but by the end of the eighteenth century, they pirated for liberty. Their controversial history provided raw material for legends.

18

Well-Told Tales

Aphantom pirate ship sailed through Newport Harbor near its crew's watery grave. An escaped pirate prisoner's heroic tale led to a poignant love story. Newport is home to a population of sea-worthy cats and a school named after a pirate. But stories about treasure left behind by Red Sea men, retired rovers and Caribbean cutthroats dominate Rhode Island's pirate legends.

Thomas Tew

In the *History of the Pirates*, Captain Charles Johnson related Thomas Tew's Madagascar adventures with Captain Mission. His account is not supported by the facts. There is, however, no reason to allow the facts to get in the way of a good story.

Captain Tew followed Mission to Libertatia and joined the pirate chief on a cruise to the Guinea coast, where Tew captured a Dutch East India Galley and an English slaver. Tew led a mission to chart the coast of Madagascar. After successfully completing that task, Captain Mission invited the Newporter on an expedition to the Arabian Sea. They captured one of the Great Mogul's ships without losing a single man and then brought the ship, its treasure and one hundred girls between the ages of twelve and eighteen back to Libertatia. Their plunder included diamonds, silks, spices, carpets and gold. Captain Tew also commanded Libertatia's fleet during a Portuguese attack. He and Mission pursued fleeing invaders.

After his successful defense of Libertatia, Captain Tew was awarded the title of admiral. Admiral Tew supervised the building of an arsenal and then sailed to the settlement of his former quartermaster and crew. During that visit, a storm wrecked Tew's ship and forced him and his crew to remain at the settlement. One morning, the presence of two sloops at anchor surprised Tew and his friends. Captain Mission had arrived.

He brought bad news. In the dead of night, the natives, without the least provocation, slaughtered all the English in Libertatia. Mission loaded the sloops with treasure and escaped. Tew told Mission about the loss of his ship. Both captains consoled each other, probably over rum and brandy. Tew wanted to return to America and Mission decided to return to Europe. Mission generously gave Tew one of his sloops, shared the treasure, and they parted company. Sadly, a storm sank Mission's sloop.

Thomas Tew Authentic Pot-Still Rum, produced by Newport Distilling Co. Tew's pirate flag design is part of the logo. *Courtesy of Newport Distilling Co.*

After he and Mission sailed out of Madagascar, Tew's tale blends with history. He arrived in Newport, agreed to go on another voyage, prepared a ship—just one—and returned to the Red Sea. An unsuccessful attack on a Muslim ship claimed Tew's life. His men surrendered.

The story of Tew's Libertatia adventure demonstrates how a legend can add flesh to the bare bones of history. It was not the only tale inspired by Tew's life.

Thomas Tew spent more time at sea than on land. There is no evidence that he owned property in Newport or married, yet stories of descendants persist. One tale involves a sea chest full of precious gems, a beautiful Moorish girl, a shipwreck, Henry David Thoreau and a pirate ghost.

In his book *True Tales and Curious Legends*, Edward Snow explained that Tew's great-great-great-great-great-granddaughter asked him to locate the pirate's treasure chest. Snow also related a tale about Tew that had never been told.

During Tew's final expedition, he captured a Moorish galleon, rescued a beautiful Moorish girl and sailed for Newport with three large chests of treasure. A violent storm overtook Tew off the Isles of Shoals near the New Hampshire coast. His ship survived only to be overcome by a hurricane. Tew's second mate washed overboard, and most of his crew got drunk and died, presumably happy, when their boat was destroyed on Boone Island's rocks off the coast of York, Maine. Tew, first mate Juan Carlos and the Moorish girl survived. One treasure chest washed ashore. Tew and Carlos buried it.

The next morning, a gunshot woke Carlos up. He rushed toward the sound and found the bloody body of his captain. The Moorish girl had killed Tew and then run off and committed suicide. Carlos found her body the next day. A passing fishing boat eventually rescued Juan Carlos. He never spoke about the buried treasure.

Carlos returned to Boone Island three years later, located the treasure chest and brought it to White's Pond, near Concord, Massachusetts. Many years later, Thoreau mentioned pirate treasure being dug up from the beach at White's Pond.

The ghost of either Tew or Juan Carlos haunts the Colonial Inn in Concord. His presence was felt as recently as the mid-twentieth century.

Snow eventually located Tew's chest, but the pirate's descendant had passed away. Snow added it to his collection. The Pirate Museum in Saint Augustine, Florida, also claims to have one of Tew's treasure chests.

Tew's Court. Members of Thomas Tew's extended family owned property on this corner behind the Newport Art Museum. *Photo by Helene Scola.*

Captain Tew did not leave behind any descendants, but his ship's mascot did. Many Newporters share their homes with the descendants of Tew's polydactyl, or many-toed, cat. Superstitious sailors considered cats to be lucky and welcomed them on board. They preferred polydactyl cats for their allegedly superior climbing and rodent-hunting skills.

Cats normally have eighteen toes—five on both front paws and four on both hind paws. Polydactyl cats can have as many as eight toes on all four paws, though that is exceedingly rare. More commonly, they have up to seven toes on one or both front paws. Occasionally they will have extra toes on one or both hind paws.

Roswell, one of Tew's cats. Both of Roswell's front paws have an extra toe resulting in a mitten-like appearance. *Photo by Helene Scola*

Their popularity as ships' cats is attested to by the fact that they are prevalent in port cities along southwest England, Wales and the east coast of North America. Polydactyl cats probably arrived in Boston Harbor, propagated and traveled up and down the coast.[64]

Ernest Hemingway's Key West, Florida home boasts a large population of these cats. A ship captain friend gave Hemingway his first polydactyl cat. All Hemingway's cats are descendants of that seaworthy feline. In Key West, they are called Hemingway's cats. In Newport, they are called Tew's cats.

Captain Thomas Paine

Thomas Paine, unlike Thomas Tew, retired in comfort. He farmed and kept pirate treasure safe for Captain Kidd and others. Treasure hunters dug around Paine's farmhouse for years. All that has been unearthed are stories about Kidd's treasure. Clauson related several in *These Plantations*.

Two nineteenth-century municipal workers digging to lay water and sewer pipes at Paine's house allegedly discovered gold, silver and ivory. Both men retired from ditch-digging, or so the story goes. There are no water or sewer lines on the north end of Jamestown, where Paine's farmhouse still stands. Residents use private wells and waste systems. Municipal workers did not discover treasure under Captain Paine's house, but someone else did.

Robert Vose purchased Captain Paine's house and farm in the late nineteenth century. He enlarged the cellar and made extensive renovations. During a visit to check on the builder's progress, one of the workmen suggested to Vose that he ask the man in charge what they found buried in Paine's backyard. Vose's builder gave him an ivory tusk and an ancient coin.

Red Sea men, including Paine's associates Kidd and Gillam, would have possessed elephant tusks. Robert Vose, a friend of Tufts University's president, donated the tusk to the school. The coin disappeared.

Soon after the discovery, the man in charge of renovations quit and paid cash for a farm of his own. He was not known to be wealthy.

Years earlier, a previous owner of Paine's farm experienced an unsettling episode. A vessel dropped anchor in front of the farmhouse. Neighbors—a seven-year-old boy and his grandmother—alarmed by the presence of the ship, knocked on the farmer's door and asked to spend the night. The farmer agreed, locked the house up, set his flintlock and axe by his side and kept watch. Sleep overtook him, however, so he did not witness the nighttime activity that took place in his front yard.

When the farmer, the boy and his grandmother awoke, they saw that the ship was gone. The farmer unlocked his front door, and they stepped outside. A deep trench had been dug just off the doorstep. Rust marks on the earth suggested that a heavy iron chest was dragged from the trench to the beach.

Captain William Kidd

It is known for certain that Captain Kidd entrusted Captain Paine with treasure, but Kidd allegedly buried loot from the Caribbean to Maine. Conanicut Island is the setting for several of those stories. Watson related one in *A Short History of Jamestown*.

During the mid-nineteenth century, a young Jamestown man, Thomas, conspired with a witch and a wizard to find buried treasure. They met in the light of a full moon. The witch told Thomas not to speak, no matter what he saw or heard. If any of them spoke, the witch's spell would be

Buried Treasure. Howard Pyle's illustration of William Kidd overseeing a treasure burial. *From Howard Pyle's* Book of Pirates.

broken, and all would be lost. The wizard's divining rod guided their progress. When the rod pointed to the earth, the witch took it and drew a circle around the spot.

While the witch danced and chanted in a bone-chilling voice, Thomas and the wizard dug inside the circle. Alerted to the coming dawn by a cock's crow, the wizard picked up his rod and aimed it into the hole. The divining rod nearly flew out of his hands. Digging with renewed vigor, throwing stones and shovelfuls of dirt out of the pit, they came to a large flat boulder, which they pried up and removed. When Thomas held the rod over the newly exposed loose earth, it jumped from his hand, sank into the soil and struck something solid. A loud metallic clank disturbed the silence.

"We found the treasure!" shouted Thomas.

He broke the spell. His disgusted companions walked away.

The young man tried to pull the divining rod out of the earth, but it would not budge. Thomas trudged home in the early dawn, slipped into his father's house and went to bed.

A story told by Botkin about Captain Kidd's buried treasure emerged thirty years after the Revolution. During a visit to Warwick, Rhode Island, Thomas Hazard noticed people digging on the beach in front of his friend's house. His friend explained that the tide unearthed a chest with a skeleton inside. It was rumored to be that of a pirate killed and buried to protect Kidd's treasure. Folks from near and far dug unsuccessfully for pirate loot. Maybe the spirit of the murdered pirate protected his captain's treasure.

The Gravelly Point Pirates

The spirits of Captain Harris and the *Ranger*'s crew have no buried treasure to protect, but they haunt their watery graves. On foggy nights, the *Ranger*'s shadowy image emerges from the mist, slips through Newport Harbor and evaporates. Moans mingled with the sound of foghorns follow the pirate ship. Its crew's restless souls are condemned to search for the *Ranger* through eternity. Night visitors to Goat Island are occasionally treated to the sight of glowing lights under the water. Are they phosphorescent marine life or the pirates' spirits?

An intriguing tale of pirate treasure connected to the Gravelly Point pirates was told by Snow in *True Tales of Pirates and Their Gold*. During the confusion following the pirates' arrest, several seamen smuggled a chest full of golden doubloons and pieces of eight off the *Greyhound* and buried it under Newport's cliffs. They made a map of the location, went to the hanging, drank their share and lost the map. A coastal storm disturbed the beach badly enough for the location of the chest to be unrecognizable. The seamen never found their buried treasure. Their descendants passed the story down as legend.

During the summer of 1949, two young women went for a walk under Newport's cliffs. Waves from a passing storm crashed along the shore. The storm washed out enough beach sand to reveal a heavy iron chest. The women described it as being about twenty inches long, twelve inches high and twelve inches wide.

The chest's cover was locked, and it was too heavy for the women to move. They abandoned their efforts. Another storm delayed their return. By the time the women went back to the beach, the chest was gone.

Maybe someone else discovered the treasure and removed it. Or is the Gravelly Point pirates' treasure still hidden under Newport's cliffs?

Governor Samuel Cranston

The treasure of enduring love was unearthed by an escaped pirate prisoner. In 1680, pirates captured and released twenty-one-year-old Samuel Cranston. Cranston was married to Mary Hart, Roger Williams's granddaughter. Their marriage united two distinguished political families. Roger Williams founded Providence, Rhode Island, and Samuel Cranston was descended from three colonial governors. Samuel's marriage to Mary helped him win Providence votes and secured Newport's status as the colonial capital.

Peterson's *History of Rhode Island* included a legendary romance about pirates capturing the governor's son. He escaped and returned home in time to prevent his wife from marrying another. Tim Cranston, the governor's descendant, and his family believe Governor Cranston's 1680 capture and release inspired the following story. Their belief is supported by the fact that the odyssey began in 1755, and its hero, Governor Cranston's son, Samuel, lived between 1681 and 1721.

The fortunes of many Newporters suffered during the French war, including those of Governor Cranston's son, Samuel. In 1755, Samuel decided to pursue business interests in the West Indies. He purchased a ship, hired a captain and crew and bid his wife farewell. It was difficult for the couple to part, but they hoped for a safe and prosperous voyage of limited duration. Both chose not to speak of the dangers Cranston faced, including piracy.

The ship arrived in the Florida Keys without incident. That happy situation ended when a low, black vessel sailed within gunshot range. Cranston's captain gathered his crew and prepared for battle.

The stranger sailed across their bow, raised the black flag and demanded complete surrender. That demand was met with fierce resistance.

The pirates' superior numbers determined the victory. They slaughtered the crew, but Cranston stood with a calm that mystified the pirate chief. Cranston's thoughts escaped to Newport and his loving wife. His demeanor won him his life, the only man to escape the pirates' murderous rampage.

Cranston's new masters took him to their island refuge and made him their slave. Any attempt to escape would have resulted in death. Freedom occupied Cranston's thoughts and dreams. He spent seven hard years on the island prison. His captors made escape impossible until an irresistible opportunity for plunder drew all the pirates off the island. Cranston was alone. His thoughts raced. Seven years of dreaming guided Cranston's escape. He fitted out a small boat and launched with a prayer for protection.

On the evening of Cranston's sixth day at sea, a sail appeared on the horizon. Cranston signaled the ship's lookout. The English merchant ship plucked Cranston out of his tiny craft and brought him to Halifax, Nova Scotia. A small sum of money, donated by the crew, allowed the Newporter to book passage for Boston, where Cranston learned his wife, believing him dead, was about to marry another man.

Empty pockets forced Cranston to walk to Newport. He was strengthened by the hope of reaching home before his wife's marriage took place. Cranston arrived in Newport thin, bedraggled and filthy. He approached his fine home pretending to be a beggar. His wife's maids took pity on him and offered him food. When Cranston asked to see their mistress, the maids told him that would not be possible. The lady was to be married that evening and had preparations to attend to.

The stranger informed Mrs. Cranston's maids he saw her husband that very day crossing at Howland's Ferry and had a message from him. Cranston refused their pleas to allow them to deliver his message and was brought to meet their mistress.

Mrs. Cranston questioned the stranger and listened attentively to the tale of her husband's capture by pirates, years of captivity and escape. Her tears of sorrow and joy reassured Cranston that he still held a place in her heart.

When his wife asked to see her husband and said she was eager to welcome him home, Cranston told her that he was near. He cleared the hair from his forehead and revealed a distinguishing scar on his brow. Husband and wife fell into each other's arms.

A wedding was held that evening, but not the one the guests expected. Mr. Russell, the groom, graciously gave way to the lawful husband of his betrothed. He led the bride down the aisle and put her hand in that of Samuel Cranston.

Simeon Potter

The names of many Newport pirates live on in history and in legend, but the name of one graced an early Newport school. In her book *The Point*, Eileen Nimmo explained that Thirty-seven Marsh Street, in Newport's Point section, was the colony's free school. Before then,

Thirty-seven Marsh Street, Newport, Rhode Island. Home of pirate Captain Simeon Potter and site of Newport's Free School. *Photo by Helene Scola.*

Potter School on Elm Street, Newport, Rhode Island, named in honor of pirate Captain Simeon Potter. *Photo by Helene Scola.*

Potter School sign. *Photo by Helene Scola.*

it was the home of Simeon Potter, a Bristol, Rhode Island pirate and *Gaspee* accomplice.

Simeon Potter made a fortune first by privateering and pirating and then in shipping and real estate. Bacon related that in 1744, Potter attacked a French fort off the African coast. He plundered a church and then burned and pillaged the town. Father Fauque, a French priest taken prisoner on Potter's ship, compared Potter's men to a band of wild monkeys.

Potter became a merchant-mariner and patriot. He helped lead the attack against the *Gaspee* and negotiated the end of Britain's siege of Bristol.

Newport outgrew its free school and built a new one on Elm Street. The city named it Potter School, in honor of the old pirate.

Treasure Hunt

Stories about Captain Kidd's treasure and pirate ghosts sparked my interest in Newport's colonial pirates. The fact that I, a native Rhode Islander, knew only the legends and none of the history surprised me. Since I could not find a book specifically about Newport's pirates, I had to hunt for information.

Books about Newport's maritime history, piracy in general and pirates of the Atlantic coast and the Red Sea fed my interest to a point. Nineteenth-century books about Newport's history gave tantalizing hints about colonial pirates, but I wanted more substantial information.

That information came, in part, from books, but primarily from colonial records, correspondence, depositions, trial accounts and newspaper articles. I dug for buried treasure—the history of Newport's colonial pirates.

Why was that history buried? When pirates victimized Newport's merchant fleet, the colony wanted to make it clear to the outlaws and to London that Newport had turned against them. Trials and executions signaled that Newport no longer welcomed pirates, but the colony also needed to change its image. Newport scuttled its reputation as a pirate haven.

In the late seventeenth and early eighteenth centuries, Newporters responded to London's Navigation Acts with attacks against Red Sea shipping. England accused the colony of piracy and harboring pirates.

By the mid-eighteenth century, Newport mariners sailed merchant ships, not pirate ships. Legitimate privateers attacked enemy vessels, not neutral commerce.

During the late eighteenth century, colonists responded to London's crippling taxes and heavy-handed enforcement tactics with attacks against His Majesty's ships in Newport Harbor. Charges of piracy resurfaced.

Newport's early colonial pirates were business partners, but its later colonial pirates were patriots. Their history is Rhode Island's history.

Notes

1. Chapin, *Privateering in King George's War*, 56. Merchantmen received Letters of Marquee, not Marquee and Reprisal, so they could claim an enemy privateer as a prize if they successfully defended themselves.
2. Jameson, *Privateering and Piracy*, 319.
3. Robson, "Newport Begins," 8:151–52.
4. Ibid., 162.
5. Hawes, *Off Soundings*, 28.
6. Chapin, "Captain Paine of Cajacet," 25–27.
7. Jameson, *Privateering and Piracy*, 223.
8. Ibid., 241.
9. Hawes, *Off Soundings*, 16.
10. Johnson, *History of the Pirates*, 53–54.
11. Records of the Colony of RI, 3:337.
12. Jameson, *Privateering and Piracy*, 218.
13. Ibid., 242–43.
14. Hawes, *Off Soundings*, 49.
15. Jameson, *Privateering and Piracy*, 241.
16. Ibid., 243.
17. Hawes, *Off Soundings*, 46.
18. Jameson, *Privateering and Piracy*, 186.
19. Ibid., 243.
20. Ibid., 176–77.
21. Records of the Colony of RI, 3:338.

22. Ibid., 337.
23. Ibid., 229.
24. Ibid., 387.
25. Artifacts and treasure can be seen at the *Whydah* Pirate Museum in Provincetown on Cape Cod.
26. Dow & Edmonds, *Pirates of the New England Coast*, 130.
27. Jameson, *Privateering and Piracy*, 318–19.
28. Ibid., 321–22.
29. Burgess, *Pirate's Pact*, 258–61.
30. Mather, *Account of the Pirates*, 42.
31. Ibid., 43.
32. *Rhode Island Historical Magazine*, 1887, 9.
33. Ibid., 1882, 163.
34. Ibid., 168.
35. Arnold, *History of the State of Rhode Island*, 2:225.
36. Johnson, *History of the Pirates*, 122.
37. Ibid.
38. Smith, *Convict's Visitor*, 2.
39. Mather, *Account of the Pirates*, 30–31.
40. Mather, *Diary of Cotton Mather*, 2:481.
41. Ibid., 490.
42. Dow and Edmonds, *Pirates of the New England Coast*, 113.
43. DeFoe, *General History of the Pyrates*, 43.
44. Bamberg and Dwyer, "Margaret (Ward) (Bradley) Wrightington, Part One," 169, 176, 178.
45. Bamberg and Dwyer, "Margaret (Ward) (Bradley) Wrightington, Part Two," 9.
46. *Trial of Thirty-Six Persons for Piracy*, 3.
47. Wikipedia.org, "Fourth Amendment."
48. *Newport Historical Society Bulletin* 146, 36.
49. Ibid., 39.
50. Staples, *Documentary History*, 3.
51. Ibid., 4.
52. Ibid., 4–5.
53. Ibid., 5.
54. Ibid., 8.
55. Ibid.
56. Ibid.
57. Ibid., 9

58. Ibid., 12.

59. Ibid., 13.

60. Ibid., 15.

61. Greene, *Short History of Rhode Island*, 222.

62. Hawes, *Off Soundings*, 101.

63. Jameson, *Privateering and Piracy*, 318–19.

64. Wikipedia.org, "Polydactyl Cats."

Selected Bibliography

Books

Andreas, Peter. *Smuggler Nation*. New York: Oxford University Press, 2013.

Arnold, Samuel Greene. *History of the State of Rhode Island and Providence Plantations*. Vols. 1–2. New York: D. Appleton & Co., 1859.

Bacon, Edgar Mahew. *Narragansett Bay*. New York: G.P. Putman's Sons, 1904.

Beal, Clifford. *Quelch's Gold*. Washington, D.C.: Potomac Books, 2008.

Bishop, Morris. *The Exotics*. New York: American Heritage Press, 1969.

Botkin, R.A., ed. *A Treasury of New England Folklore*. New York: Crown Publishers, 1947.

Burgess, Douglas R. *The Pirate's Pact*. New York: McGraw Hill, 2008.

Chapin, Howard M. *Privateering in King George's War*. Providence, RI: E.A. Johnson Co., 1928.

Clauson, J. Earl. *These Plantations*. Providence, RI: Roger Williams Press, 1937.

Clifford, Barry. *Expedition Whydah*. New York: Cliff Street Books, 1999.

Cordingly, David. *Under the Black Flag*. New York: Harcourt Brace and Co., 1995.

DeFoe, Daniel. *A General History of the Pyrates*. Edited by Manuel Schonhorn. New York: Dover Publications, 1972.

Dow, George Francis, and John Henry Edmonds. *The Pirates of the New England Coast, 1630–1730*, 1923. Reprint, New York: Dover Publications, 1996.

Ellms, Charles. *The Pirates: Authentic Narratives of the Lives, Exploits, and Executions of the World's Most Infamous Buccaneers.* Published as *The Pirates' Own Book*, 1837. Reprint, New York: Gramercy Books, 1996.

Gosse, Philip. *The History of Piracy.* New York: Dover Publications, 2007.

Greene, George W. *A Short History of Rhode Island.* Providence, RI: J.A. & R.A. Reid, Publishers,1877.

Hattendorf, John. *Semper Eadem: A History of Trinity Church in Newport, 1698–2000.* Newport, RI: Trinity Church, 2001.

Hawes, Alexander Boyd. *Off Soundings.* Chevy Chase, MD: Posterity Press, 1999.

Jameson, John Franklin, ed. *Privateering and Piracy in the Colonial Period.* New York: MacMillan Co., 1923.

James, Sydney, V. *Colonial Rhode Island.* New York: Scribner's, 1975.

Johnson, Captain Charles. *The History of the Pirates.* Norwich, UK. Reprint, R. Hubbard, 1814. (Originally printed in London.)

Mather, Cotton. *Diary of Cotton Mather.* Vols. 1–2. New York: Frederick Ungar, 1957.

Nimmo, Eileen G. *"The Point" of Newport, Rhode Island.* Newport, RI: J&E Publishing, 2001.

Paine, Ralph D. *The Book of Buried Treasure.* New York: Arno Press, 1981.

Peterson, Edward. *History of Rhode Island.* New York: John S. Taylor, 1853.

Pringle, Patrick. *Jolly Roger.* New York: W.W. Norton & Co., 1953.

Raven, Rory. *Burning the Gaspee.* Charleston, SC: The History Press, 2012.

Rediker, Marcus. *Between the Devil and the Deep Blue Sea.* New York: Cambridge University Press, 1987.

———. *Villains of All Nations.* Boston: Boston Press, 2004.

Ritchie, Ethel Colt. *Block Island Lore and Legends.* Block Island, RI: Mrs. Frances M. Nugent, 1970.

Ritchie, Robert C. *Captain Kidd and the War against the Pirates.* Cambridge, MA: Harvard University Press, 1986.

Scott, E. Jean. *A Few of the Tews of Newport, RI.* Middletown, RI, 1994.

Seay, Scott D. *Hanging between Heaven and Earth.* Champaign: Illinois University Press, 2009.

Sheffield, William P. *Privateersmen of Newport, Address of William P. Sheffield before the Rhode Island Historical Society in Providence, February 7, 1882.* Providence: Rhode Island Historical Society, 1883.

Smith, William. *The Convicts' Visitor.* Newport, RI: Peter Edes, 1791.

Snow, Edward Rowe. *Pirates and Buccaneers of the Atlantic Coast.* Reprint. Boston: Commonwealth Editions, 2004.

———. *True Tales and Curious Legends.* New York: Dodd, Meade & Co., 1969.

———. *True Tales of Pirates and Their Gold.* New York: Dodd, Mead & Co., 1953.

Staples, William R. *The Documentary History of the Destruction of the* Gaspee. Providence, RI: Knowles, Vose and Anthony, 1845.

Watson, Walter Leon. *A Short History of Jamestown.* Providence, RI: J.F. Greene Co., 1933.

Weeks, Lyman Horace, ed. *An Historical Digest of the Provincial Press 1689–1783.* The MA Series, vol. 1, 1689–1707. New York: Curtiss-Way Co., 1911.

Wilkins, Harold T. *Captain Kidd and His Skeleton Island.* New York: Liveright Publishing Co., 1937.

Zacks, Richard. *The Pirate Hunter: The True Story of Captain Kidd.* New York: Hyperion Books, 2002.

Web Sources

Wikipedia.org. "The Fourth Amendment." http:Wikipedia.org/wiki/Fourth Amendment.

———. "Polydactyl Cats." http:Wikipedia.org/wiki/Polydactyl-cat.

Journals

Appleton, Marguerite. "Rhode Island's First Court of Admiralty." *New England Quarterly* (January 1932): 148–58.

Bamberg, Cherry Fletcher, FASG, and Michael F. Dwyer. "Margaret (Ward) (Bradley) Wrightington, Part One." *Rhode Island Roots* (December 2012).

———. "Margaret (Ward) (Bradley) Wrightington, Part Two." *Rhode Island Roots* (March 2013).

Bosco, Ronald A. "Lectures at the Pillory: The Early American Execution Sermon." *American Quarterly* 30 (1978): 156–76.

Chapin, Howard M. "Captain Paine of Cajacet." *Rhode Island Historical Society Collections* 23 (January 1930): 19–32.

Minnick, Wayne C. "The New England Execution Sermon, 1639–1800." *Speech Monographs* 35 (1963): 77–89.

Newport Historical Society Bulletin 146 (1972): 36–9.

Rhode Island Historical Magazine 7 (April 1887).

Rhode Island Historical Magazine 3 (July 1882).

Rhode Island History Magazine (October 1885).

Robson, Lloyd A. "Newport Begins." *Newport Historical Society Bulletin* (1964).

Williams, D.E. "Puritans and Pirates." *Early American Literature* 22 (1987): 233–51.

Primary Sources

Emlyn, Sollom, ed. *A Complete Collection of State Trials and Proceedings upon High Treason and Other Crimes and Misdemeanors.* England, 1730.

Mather, Cotton. *An Account of the Pirates with Divers of Their Speeches, etc.* Boston, 1723.

———. *An Essay upon Remarkables in the Way of Wicked Men: A Sermon on the Tragical End unto Which the Way of Twenty-Six Pirates Brought Them; At New Port on Rhode Island, July 19, 1723.* Boston, 1723.

Records of the Colony of Rhode Island. Vols. 3–4.

Rhode Island General Treasurer Accounts 1712–1713, 141–42, 144–45, 150, 179.

Rhode Island Public Notary Records. Vol. 4, 1721–41, 414, 418, 471.

Trial of Thirty-Six Persons for Piracy. Boston, 1723.

Index

About the Author

G loria Merchant's degrees in art history and art education led to a rich and varied career. Memberships in the Newport Historical Society, Redwood Library & Athenaeum and Preservation Society of Newport County nourish her interest in local history. Gloria grew up on Narragansett Bay. She and her husband have sailed the bay and beyond for over forty years and know its waters as well as Newport's colonial pirates did.

Gloria Merchant in the library of the Seamen's Church Institute, Newport, Rhode Island. *Photo by Helene Scola.*